Your Mother
Was Right

Your Mother Was Right

All the Great Advice You Tried to Forget

kate reardon

FOUNDER OF TOPTIPS.COM

THREE RIVERS PRESS • NEW YORK

Published in the United States by Three Rivers Press,
an imprint of the Crown Publishing Group,
a division of Random House, Inc., New York.
www.crownpublishing.com

Three Rivers Press and the Tugboat design are
registered trademarks of Random House, Inc.

Portions of this work have been previously published
online on the website www.TopTips.com

Library of Congress Cataloging-in-Publication Data
Reardon, Kate.
    Your mother was right : all the great advice you tried to forget /
by Kate Reardon. — 1st ed.
        p. cm.
    1. Women—Conduct of life. 2. Girls—Conduct of life. I. Title.
    BJ1610.R434 2010
    646.70082—dc22

                                                    2010000683

ISBN 978-0-307-58863-0

Printed in the United States of America

Illustrations by Mary Lynn Blasutta

10 9 8 7 6 5 4 3 2 1

First Edition

For my friends.
Thank you for letting me pick you.

contents

*Your Mother
Was Right*

Introduction

There are two types of women: those who are a bit vague and noncommittal when you ask what delicious perfume they're wearing, and those who, when they discover an exciting new method of hair removal, demand that you feel their newly smooth lower leg and examine it minutely for any vestiges of hair as they dial the salon to make an appointment for you.

The website TopTips.com is very much for and written by the latter sort of woman. The site is a community of women who don't feel that life is a giant competition, and that another woman's success (whether it be at work or at hair removal) diminishes them in any way. It attracts women who actually like other women, and who enjoy giving each other advice.

Welcome to *Your Mother Was Right*, the second book of practical, funny, and brilliant tips gleaned from TopTips.com. Since the first book was published, tens of thousands more tips have been submitted to the site, so we thought it would be crazy not to put the best together into a second volume. There are even more hard-won words of wisdom on an extraordinary range of subjects, from how to calm a screaming baby to how to react when you find naughty texts on your partner's cell phone, how to make perfect meatballs, and how to find a suitable mate in later life. And there are two new and exciting categories that apply to everyone: friendship and happiness.

Most of the problems posted on the site prompt two or three tipsters to post solutions. But the question, How to be happy? has elicited (at the time of going to press) an awesome 113 answers. Happiness is the one thing we all crave, and evidently it's the one thing about which most people feel they have some good counsel to share. So, thus inspired, we launched the Campaign for Happiness to disperse some of this wonderful advice; scores of celebrities shared their tips, the press gleefully reported our efforts, and every day we suggested a simple act of happiness for everyone to commit.

The Friendship chapter (covering everything from how to be a good friend to how to cope when things aren't going so well) was prompted by the following exchange: Someone posted the problem, "How to turn little friendships into true ones when you need a shoulder to cry on?" I was delighted when a tipster called Pienkfly replied, "Let me give you the perfect answer. We at Top Tips are your *true* best friends. We are here 24/7. So if you need to cry, we are just a click away. I subscribed to this website 18 March 2008, and you know what? I submitted my problems, and got so many true, straight answers and solutions. Although we don't know each other, we give you honest help. Some friends lie to one another just to make them feel better; we don't."

One of the benefits of TopTips.com is that it's anonymous—you can discuss anxieties you wouldn't dare voice even to your best friend. Written and read by a community of women from all over the world, it allows you to post problems (from the prosaic to the profound), and those with a view pile in with their suggested solutions. Encouraging you to leave something handy behind when you go, TopTips.com is the ultimate interactive advice column.

This book is the result of a collaboration among the thousands of women who have submitted advice on TopTips.com. Editing it was simple, but not easy: Starting with a spreadsheet of the 26,409 tips that have been submitted since we compiled the last book, I whittled it down to about 800. Which was tough—there were so many brilliant tips that it was incredibly hard to choose. Those that were heartbreaking to delete I'm saving for the next book.

I ended up picking ones that answered my own questions or made the most sense. A word of warning: I haven't tested them all so if you follow any of the advice, think it through first. If a tip doesn't work, or you end up turning your toenails green, please let me and the rest of the world know by going to TopTips.com—so we can get it right for the reprint.

As you are now the proud owner of a copy of *Your Mother Was Right: All the Great Advice You Tried to Forget* and presumably have read at least some of it, you are entitled to enhanced status when you register on TopTips.com. How cool is that? Simply enter the word *genius* in the Promotional Code field and you will automatically be flagged as something of a guru within the TopTips.com community.

Beauty

or It's not all in the eye of the beholder.

Beauty maintenance is a never-ending task. You can view it as terrifically dull, or you can believe that it is pampering, "me time." Whatever your attitude and whether you are a nail-clippers-and-hairbrush sort of girl or someone with a more elaborate routine, it is a fact that no matter what you do, you will only have to do it all over again sometime later. All tasks are eventually futile; body hair and nails grow relentlessly and all we can do is try to head them off at the pass with an arsenal of ever-more-sophisticated products and devices. The most wonderful hairstyle in the world will at some point have to be shampooed, and makeup will have to be removed. And yet . . . most women take an intrinsic pleasure in grooming themselves. Whether it is done to ensnare a man or not, don't talk to them about it. Almost all men experience a boredom bordering on narcolepsy when women start talking about makeup; as far as they're concerned, Mascara is a soccer player. And for them it is an insoluble mystery about the nature of time itself why no woman can accurately say how long she will take when makeup is involved.

HOW TO GET THE MOST FROM EXPENSIVE FACE CREAMS

Make sure that prior to applying your face cream your face is completely dry. If your skin is at all damp, it will dilute the product.

Sophie08

HOW TO NOT LOOK TIRED

Try massaging your ears with your thumb and forefinger. Start at the top and massage firmly all over your ears and earlobes. Do it whenever you need to perk up! Sounds silly, but it works.

Dusty

HOW TO CLEAN TWEEZERS

Sanitize them in boiling water and if they really are scrungy around the tips, a Brillo pad works wonders. Especially good on slant-ended tweezers.

distractedhousewife

HOW TO SAVE ON FACIAL MASKS AND HAVE GLOSSY HAIR

My mother always used egg whites as a facial mask, and she'd apply the yolk to her hair to make it look glossy. Nothing wasted—everything gained.

housegoose

HOW TO MAKE A NATURAL BATH OIL

Get a bottle of almond oil from the drugstore (it's very cheap) and add a few drops of your favorite essential oils—my personal favorites are rose, lavender, and geranium. Shake up and pour a few drops in your bath!

Alternatively, pop a few sprigs of rosemary or lavender in your bottle of almond oil, close tightly, and let infuse for a week or so—you will end up with a lovely bath oil. You could decant it into a pretty bottle and display it in your bathroom or use as a gift.

Make sure you use only woody, tough herbs for this (like rosemary and lavender); things like rose petals or fruit peel will turn nasty and discolored.

sarahfairy

HOW TO MAKE A FACE MASK FOR OILY SKIN

Milk of magnesia is excellent for oily and acne-prone skin; you will see a difference almost immediately. Apply every night using a cotton ball, let it dry for ten minutes, and then wash off as normal.

friqbal

HOW TO IMPROVE THE APPEARANCE OF EARLOBES
STRETCHED FROM WEARING HEAVY EARRINGS

Wearing heavy dangling earrings over a long time can cause your earlobe piercings to stretch. This looks horrible, and lots of women opt for earlobe surgery later in life. You can "fix" it invisibly: Just cut a small piece of surgical tape or a Band-Aid, big enough to cover the hole, and place it on the back of the earlobe. Then carefully put your earring stem through the tape support. It is as if you had a brand new piercing. Change it daily.

Lesley998

HOW TO GET THAT PERFECT EYEBROW SHAPE

Have them tattooed by an expert, either permanently or semi-permanently. If the former, don't go for too dark a color as they must match your skin as time goes by. The process hurts like hell but there are products you can get to numb the skin beforehand, and it's really worth it.

Cali

HOW TO APPLY FALSE EYELASHES

Don't put the glue directly onto the false lashes; instead put a small blob onto the back of your hand and then lightly slide or pull your false lashes through it. This stops you from using too much glue.

PinkFluffyDee

HOW TO USE EYELASH CURLERS

Instead of just holding down with your curlers once on each lash, do it three times, holding for about fifteen seconds each time, starting from the very base, then the middle, and then the tips.

frankieface

HOW TO CALM PUFFY EYES AFTER CRYING

Take a washcloth and rinse it with very cold water. Place it over your eyes and rinse it again in cold water as needed.

Jillaroo95

HOW TO APPLY EYELINER WITHOUT SMUDGING

When you put on eyeliner, rest the elbow of your applying arm on a dressing table or other flat, stable surface. It will help keep your hand steady and the line neater. Also, try a felt-tip applicator instead of liquid and brush; it's easier to get neat.

peony

Don't use eye cream before applying eyeliner. If you must use something, try a gel that is less oily and less likely to cause smudges.

Apply a thin line of your face powder with a stiff, angled eyeliner brush around your eye; then apply your eyeliner over the top.

sarahfairy

I use an eyebrow pencil instead; it doesn't smudge as easily and stays put longer.

Marrant

HOW TO SHARPEN EYELINER PENCILS WITHOUT
BREAKING THEM

Put them in the freezer for a minute or two before sharpening. Works great.

jess5377

HOW TO FIND AN EYE SHADOW BASE THAT ACTUALLY KEEPS ITS PROMISE

I usually use my foundation as a base. You can dab as much as you want with your finger all over your eyelid or just where you need it. It's affordable and it works.

hoopz

HOW TO MAKE YOUR EYES LOOK BIGGER

Use a light-color eye shadow in the inner corner of your eye, and get darker as you go further out. Also use eyelash curlers; they really open up your eyes.

xxHazeLxx

Use white eye pencil on the inner lower lids. It will highlight your eye color, too.

Marrant

HOW TO KNOW WHEN YOU'RE WEARING TOO MUCH MAKEUP

Face a window and look into a mirror. You will be able to see if you have put on too much foundation.

lemonlips123

HOW TO LOOK GREAT ON A BUDGET

With mascara I've found it's how you prepare the lash that adds drama as some of the most expensive mascaras don't live up to their claims. Use eyelash curlers to give your lashes great curl, then build up the coats of mascara, separating each with a good lash comb.

Marrant

HOW TO LOOK YOUNGER

The easiest, cheapest, fastest way to look younger is to stand up straight. You can take ten years off your look by pulling your shoulders down and your stomach in. Make this a habit when you walk down the street and no matter how old you are, it will take years off.

kathconn

HOW TO SET FOUNDATION

Wait a good five minutes between putting on your moisturizer and applying your foundation. Makes a big difference and will give you a better canvas to build on.

pinkbunnygirl

HOW TO STOP LIPSTICK FROM BLEEDING

When putting on your makeup, apply your base foundation to your lips as well. This will prevent the lipstick from bleeding.

micheleo810

HOW TO GET GORGEOUS CUTICLES

Rub a drop of olive oil into each cuticle.

chocolatenoor

HOW TO GROW LONG, STRONG NAILS

Try taking glucosamine supplements daily. They're relatively inexpensive and if you take them every day, within a month your nails will be noticeably stronger (your skin and hair will be better too!).

Myspandex

HOW TO GUARD AGAINST SMUDGING YOUR PEDICURE

It's simple, but easily forgotten: for pedicures, wear flip-flops to the salon.

LindaCee

HOW TO TAKE CARE OF YOUR NAILS

Have manicures and pedicures but with no polish—natural and healthy looking, better for your nails, and no excruciating waiting time while they dry.

LauraBailey

HOW TO MAINTAIN A GREAT MANICURE/PEDICURE

Before you paint your nails, even if you don't need to remove old polish, go over them with a cotton pad soaked in nail polish remover. This removes any traces of dirt, oil, soap, hand cream, etc., which otherwise would stop the polish from adhering properly to your nails.

njdavie2

HOW TO MAKE ACRYLIC OVERLAYS LAST LONGER

Use nail oil! As soon as you get back from the salon, massage lots in and around your nails and cuticles; this seems to stop any cracking or lifting. Repeat every night if you can. And whenever you are using bleach, and other household cleaners wear rubber gloves, as that stuff will permeate your nails in no time and make the overlays lift off!

blondearieschick

HOW TO STOP BITING YOUR NAILS

Take up a handicraft such as knitting so when you're in front of the TV, your hands are kept busy.

elizabethevelyn

Try giving up a nail at a time.

LexieLou

I've bitten my nails my whole life and this is the only thing that has worked: Buy a big pack of cheap false nails (I got one from my local beauty store with ten sets in the pack) and wear them. Cut them short and paint them so they look natural and you can still use your hands. Change the nails every three days and by the time you've used up all of the sets, your own nails will have grown.

caramelfrapp

Every morning after eating breakfast, scrape your nails (even if minute, they do exist) along a bar of soap and then go about your day. Every time you go to bite your nails, you'll get a disgusting taste in your mouth. This also prevents dirt from getting trapped under your nails.

NatureFirst

HOW TO STOP TINY AIR BUBBLES FROM APPEARING
AFTER APPLYING THE TOP COAT OF NAIL POLISH

Don't put too much nail polish on the brush and apply it slowly.

queenbee231

HOW TO CLEAR UP ACNE

I used to suffer with acne and tried every kind of lotion and potion until it dawned on me that a natural remedy would be best. I've done lots of research and found out that a honey face mask works wonders! Simple as that: Smear honey over your whole face, leave for twenty minutes, and wash off with water. Within a few weeks you really notice the difference.

browngirl

Tea tree oil contains terpinen-4-ol, which fights harmful bacteria and fungi. This ingredient makes tea tree oil an effective treatment against acne.

Callista

HOW TO PREVENT WRINKLES AROUND YOUR EYES

Smear a good layer of Vaseline round your eyes at night. It totally works.

Jemzie

HOW TO GET WHITER TEETH AS NATURALLY AS POSSIBLE

Dip your brush into baking soda and brush your teeth. This is a little abrasive and removes coffee and red wine stains.

Redlady

HOW TO GET FOOD OUT OF YOUR TEETH WHEN YOU'RE AT THE OFFICE AND DON'T HAVE ANY FLOSS

On those awful occasions when I have gotten food caught in my teeth and haven't had any floss on hand, I've used . . . a staple. Really. Punch the stapler once to release a staple and use that.

Jillaroo95

Body

or Either do something about it or shut up.

Who thinks they've got the perfect body? I bet nobody. Sure, we can all see that we've got good bits, if we look really hard, but very few women are satisfied with what they've got. So we complain ad nauseam. After one such bout of mindless, self-defeating, not in the slightest way interesting to anybody (even myself) droning, my brother turned to me and said, "If it really bothered you that much, you'd do something about it." It was a Damascene moment—I hadn't dieted or exercised; ergo, I was clearly happy enough with my body. I immediately stopped complaining about it. And by removing those words from my own mouth, satisfaction with my own shape became a (mute) self-fulfilling prophecy. What we say is what we think (if you don't believe me, try not thinking in words), and what we think is what we feel. I highly recommend it.

HOW TO BE CONFIDENT WITH YOUR BODY, ESPECIALLY WHEN NAKED IN FRONT OF SOMEONE SPECIAL

Remember the rule of thumb. Look at your thumb now and what do you see? Just a thumb, right? OK, so it might be a little short, or the nail might not be filed to perfection, but really, it's just a thumb. Now when you are naked in front of your partner, just remember your thumb, and remember that he's not seeing your short bits or big bits or little bits or whatever, he's just praising the Lord that there is a naked woman, no matter what she looks like, standing in front of him.

princess mischa

HOW TO BEAT CELLULITE

This won't stop the problem but if you do it long enough it will help: Before leaving your shower, spray your cellulite area with really cold water for as long as you can bear.

Helloimcharli

With a dry body brush, brush your body with upward strokes toward your heart, then exfoliate in the shower and moisturize when you get out.

vbullimore

Always use a body moisturizer after your bath or shower. Doesn't have to be an expensive one; baby oil will do. When you rub the cream/lotion/oil/whatever in, rub vigorously. Make a fist and rub with your knuckles. Do it for about a minute on each area. It won't go overnight, but keep at it and I promise it will really help. Drink loads of water! Run up stairs, and walk rather than going by car.

AKB

I bought some vitamin E oil three days ago and have been massaging it into my damn thighs morning and night, and it's made a pronounced difference in my cellulite already. Cellulite is a skin problem, *not* a weight problem, and the vitamin E seems to really help. I also take it as a supplement, and see a big difference when I drink a lot of water, so keep refilling the glasses!

BooBoo

Scoot along your carpet on your butt fifty times—it makes the blood circulate and is really effective.

rileyko5

HOW TO PREVENT STRETCH MARKS

My mom (God rest her soul) told me that the best way to prevent stretch marks is to massage in extra virgin olive oil. She had five children, no stretch marks, and great skin at eighty-six.

milou

HOW TO APPLY SELF-TANNER TO YOUR BACK WHEN YOU'VE GOT NOBODY TO HELP

Apply as much of the tanner as you can on your lower back, the back of your shoulders, etc. using your palm, then use the back of your hand to rub it in the middle/top area of your back. It works for me—although I don't think that clicking noise in my shoulder is normal, eek!

TashNU53

HOW TO REMOVE SELF-TANNER WITHOUT SCRUBBING

Acetone (nail polish remover) usually does the trick.

Chessy2

Use hair removal cream; it removes self-tanner from legs and also removes hairs, so you get a two-in-one bonus!

anniebell

HOW TO CALM ITCHY HAIR REGROWTH AFTER EPILATION

It helps to exfoliate the day before hair removal. If you do get itchy skin though, a cotton ball soaked with witch hazel works to cool and calm and is very cheap. (Also works great on zits.)

pickledparsnip

HOW TO BEAT SHAVING RASH

If you shave your legs when you are slightly cold you will probably have goose bumps, and shaving will damage the skin; therefore you will have itchy, broken skin afterward. So the next time you shave, make sure that you are warm.

Boo

HOW TO GET A SUPERSMOOTH SHAVE ON YOUR LEGS

To achieve supersmooth legs, take a warm bath to soften the hairs, exfoliate, then use a little olive oil (instead of shaving gel). This works wonders. The razor will glide smoothly, leaving legs free of cuts, and they'll feel really well moisturized afterward.

AlixGB

Run your hands up your legs to feel (rather than look) for any remaining hair or rough bits.

Evanescence100

HOW TO MAKE DRY HANDS SOFT

I use almond oil to soften my hands. It does wonders for your nails by preventing them from splitting and cracking. Just apply a small drop and rub in well at night and after any contact with water containing detergent. It's very inexpensive and available at most drugstores.

Kgirl

HOW TO MAKE YOUR HANDS SMOOTH AND PREVENT THEM FROM BLEEDING IN COLD WEATHER

I've had this problem for years and I know it is *extremely* painful! Try using a castor oil/zinc cream (or any other cream for babies' butts) just before bedtime. Cover up with the plastic gloves from a home hair-coloring kit. The plastic makes your hands sweat a lot, but they absorb the cream better. Try not to do this only when your hands are bleeding, but as a special weekly treatment all year long.

Jilly14

HOW TO GET RID OF CORNS OR CALLUSES

Wrap a Band Aid around the affected toes at all times when wearing shoes or slippers. Never cut corns or calluses or rub them with pumice stones or files. I did beauty therapy for nine years and know that corns and calluses are ways your feet or hands protect themselves from friction, so if you apply friction by rubbing them they will never go away. Just wrap them in ordinary Band Aids all the time, even if you're going to the corner store. I have tried this and it works wonders. The skin will normalize when it realizes pressure is no longer applied to it. Be patient; it could take up to a year, depending on the size of the corn.

deannadollson

HOW TO GET SOFT FEET

After you have done your pedicure and slathered your feet in moisturizer, wrap your feet in plastic wrap and put on a pair of old socks. If you can bear it, sleep in them. If not, wear for a couple of hours—your feet will be amazingly soft.

JoMalone

HOW TO CURE SKIN THAT BRUISES EASILY

It's helpful to take a vitamin B supplement. They come in various strengths, and I've noticed an improvement in my healing since I began to take it.

ashling

HOW TO FIND A LAUNDRY SOAP THAT IS GOOD FOR SENSITIVE SKIN

Try a laundry soap for baby clothing as it is always good for sensitive skin.

Sassy

HOW TO STOP THIGHS FROM RUBBING AND CHAFING
WHEN WEARING A SKIRT IN HOT WEATHER

Talcum powder should do the trick.

mackieox

HOW TO CURE OR PREVENT A RASH UNDER A HEAVY BUST

Get yourself fitted for a new bra—the girls should *not* be hanging down against the skin below (and I say this as a GG-cupper who had exactly this problem when wearing the wrong size in the past).

distractedhousewife

Tightening your bra straps helps with this problem. I see it in a lot of expectant moms and I just adjust the straps.

spooner

HOW TO ENJOY YOUR BREASTS AND DRESS SEXILY
WITHOUT MAKING MEN FEEL UNCOMFORTABLE

The secret is to make sure you're wearing a really good bra that "contains" your breasts. You can then wear low-cut tops and dresses without that horrible wobbly spillage. As for making men uncomfortable, I'm afraid some men are born with their eyes attached by invisible strings to the nearest pair of boobs.

They can't help themselves; the string keeps pulling their eyes back to them! It's often not their fault, and they may mean nothing sinister by it.

Basically, it's about choosing the right time and place to flash the flesh. A night out on the town? Yes. A Wednesday morning in the office? No.

LindaCee

HOW TO PREVENT PEOPLE FROM STARING AT YOUR CHEST

You could try saying, "Oh! Have I spilled something on my top?"

atopgirl

Cooking

or This has never happened to me before, I promise.

You're either a cook or a cookee. There are those for whom cooking is a grand passion and those who think it's largely a waste of time and effort when all we need is fuel. Not being able to cook is one of the great levelers; like medication and heartbreak, it's one of the few things that unites all social classes. However, even if you're not a sensational cook, it can be hard to resist the lure of baking cookies—which is a different matter entirely. Baking is the ultimate in soothing therapy: It's basic, it rarely involves sharp knives and baffling instructions, and it's always about treats.

HOW TO AVOID LUMPS IN WHITE SAUCE

Sift the flour as you add it—this helps prevent lumps from forming in the first place. If you do get lumps, whisk the sauce before adding more liquid, and it should come out smooth.

meredith tangle

HOW TO AVOID SPATTERING WHEN FRYING

Before frying, pat the food dry with a paper towel. Dry food always browns nicely. Also, try not to use too much cooking oil.

cherylsaigeon

HOW TO COOK A FULL BREAKFAST WHILE YOU GET READY FOR WORK

Put bacon, sausages, tomatoes, and mushrooms in a roasting pan and drizzle with oil. Cook in the oven for fifteen minutes while you shower and dress. Turn the sausages and bacon, crack eggs into spaces in the pan, and put back in the oven for ten to fifteen minutes more. Make toast and put on your lipstick. Bada-bing, bada-boom!

distractedhousewife

HOW TO COOK EGGPLANT SO IT MELTS IN THE MOUTH

It's not the cooking method, it's the preparation. Eggplant needs to be "sweated" so it is less tough and bitter. Put some paper towels on a plate. Slice the eggplant about 1/3 inch thick, then salt the slices on both sides and place them on the paper towels. Layer the slices with paper towels in between each layer and on top. Then put another plate on top of the whole thing and something on top to weigh it all down, and stick it in the refrigerator. Do this in the morning, and at dinnertime you'll have tender eggplant that you can cook any way you like.

Jillaroo95

HOW TO COOK BASMATI RICE SO IT'S NOT STICKY AND OVERCOOKED

Our Chinese amah in Singapore taught me this technique fifty years ago. It is completely foolproof. Put the rice in lots of boiling water and cook for fourteen minutes. (It should still be covered in water.) Pour through a sieve and immediately run cold water over the rice until it is cold. Cover and leave until serving time. Then pour a kettleful of boiling water through it and serve. Result: large, fluffy, dry grains with a minimum of starch.

Canopus

HOW TO COOK THE PERFECT SOFT-BOILED EGG

I put the egg (room temperature) in a pan of cold water and bring to a boil, timing it for two minutes once the water is bubbling. This is perfect for a soft-boiled medium-sized egg. Add thirty seconds for a large egg. Also, slice off the top right after removing the egg from the water; otherwise it will keep cooking. If it's slightly too runny, pop the sliced-off top back on and leave for a minute or so; it will cook a little more and should be just right.

meredith tangle

HOW TO DELICIOUSLY AND HEALTHILY COOL DOWN
HOT OATMEAL

In the summer when fresh fruit is plentiful, lightly rinse, dry, and coarsely chop lots of it and freeze. In the cooler months, if you're making hot cereal, pop a few slices of frozen fruit or frozen berries into the cereal. It serves the dual purpose of cooling the oatmeal enough to eat and adding flavor, fiber, and color to your breakfast.

CeeVee

HOW TO EASILY AND QUICKLY REMOVE FAT FROM SOUPS OR GRAVY

Heat the soup until very hot. Pour it into a heatproof bowl or large measuring cup such as Pyrex and then cover the surface with ice cubes. Wait three to five minutes and give things a gentle stir. You'll find that the fat has solidified into little globules and is clinging to the ice cubes. Remove and discard the ice cubes and you've removed the vast majority of the fat.

CeeVee

Leave overnight in the fridge. The fat will rise to the top and you can skim it off. This is useful with stews and casseroles, too. They often taste better the next day anyway.

patsharp

HOW TO EASILY CUT ANY LARGE QUANTITY OF RAW MEAT

Stick the meat in the freezer for twenty minutes before cutting it. This makes it much easier to cut and to trim away the fat.

CeeVee

HOW TO EAT HEALTHILY ON A TIGHT BUDGET

Check your butcher and supermarket for meat sales and freeze the extra portions. If you like peas and beans, cook them as an inexpensive protein option. Get a slow cooker if you can. They're cheap to run, can be ignored while cooking, and will make tougher ends of meat tender. They're the best kitchen investment you can make for efficiency and economy.

ashling

HOW TO FIND OR COOK TASTY FOOD THAT IS LOW IN SALT OR SODIUM

Lots of herb and spice mixes are marketed as salt replacers; Spike is a good one. Also, cook with garlic—good for the heart and adds wonderful flavor to food.

Jillaroo95

HOW TO GET ALL THE BITS OF SHELL OUT OF SEAFOOD

If you have to sort through crabmeat or lobster to pick out the random bits of shell, spread the meat out on a cookie sheet and stick it in a 350°F oven for just three or four minutes. All the shell bits will turn opaque and be easy to see and pick out! (This doesn't actually cook the meat.)

CeeVee

HOW TO GET CRACKLING CRISP WHEN ROASTING PORK

Score the fat and then rub with oil and salt. Really crispy crackling!

Redlady

HOW TO GET ONION OR GARLIC SMELL OFF YOUR HANDS

A catering trade secret: Wash your hands afterward in white wine or vinegar (if you don't mind that smell!).

Abi1973

HOW TO GET RID OF CHILE BURNS ON YOUR HANDS
AFTER CHOPPING FRESH CHILES

The antidote for chile is sugar. Dilute some in warm water and soak your hands in it, then rub in Vaseline.

Ali161

HOW TO GRATE CHEESE, CHOCOLATE, ETC. NEATLY

Place the grater inside a plastic bag and grate in there. Voila! The grated food is contained and there's no mess to clean up.

CeeVee

HOW TO JAZZ UP STORE-BOUGHT PASTA SAUCE

Cheese sauces—add a couple of sprinkles of dried sage and a tiny pinch of rosemary.

Tomato sauces—shake in some red pepper flakes (how much depends on how spicy you like your food), add some dried or chopped fresh basil or oregano, and grind in lots of black pepper.

Top with freshly grated Parmesan and a couple of fresh basil leaves.

sarahfairy

If adding fresh ingredients is too time-consuming for you, the easiest trick in the book for tomato-based sauces is to add a few drops of Tabasco and season well.

Leilu

HOW TO KEEP ASPARAGUS FRESH

Lay your asparagus flat on a couple of paper towels. Place a couple more paper towels on top and roll up the asparagus jelly-roll style, making sure that the tips are an inch or so inside the towels. Place in a plastic bag—you can use the one you brought them home in—and they will last for up to two weeks.

scherzo9

HOW TO EXTEND THE LIFE OF FRESH HERBS

Mix finely chopped herbs with olive oil and freeze in an ice cube tray to use at a later date.

Tooke

Stand them in a large glass of water. Put a small plastic bag over the glass and secure with a tight elastic band. Even difficult herbs like cilantro will last for a week or more and stay fresh.

patsharp

HOW TO MAKE CHILDREN'S PACKED LUNCHES
INTERESTING

Try letting the kids help you shop for the food in the super-market. That way, they get a say in what they eat and in what goes into their lunch boxes. Obviously, you have to put your foot down when they choose something unsuitable, but overall children feel that because they have chosen their food them-selves, they should eat it. Also, try letting them help prepare their sandwiches and other foods. I used to find that hav-ing my veggies cut into interesting shapes made them more interesting. A Top Tip is to write a little note to pop into the lunch box saying, "I hope you like your sandwich" or "Cutting those vegetable shapes was fun" or—the best one—a simple "I love you."

elle_c_BFFL

When I was little my mom used to write a message for me on my banana, which my friends and I thought was hilarious!

Marie5991

HOW TO MAKE A ROAST SUPERTENDER

Whatever method you use, never cook meat straight from the fridge. A large piece of beef will need at least half an hour at room temperature before going into the oven. And all meat needs to stand for at least ten minutes before carving.

milou

HOW TO MAKE PERFECT MEATBALLS

Perhaps not perfect, but certainly no-fuss and supertasty: Buy a pack of high-quality sausages. Snip at both ends, then squeeze roughly a third of the way down the sausage so that the meat comes away from the casing. Repeat until you have three "meatballs" from each sausage. Roll them between your hands if you insist on their being perfect, although I find that they come out roughly the right shape anyway.

Leilu

HOW TO MINIMIZE THE AMOUNT OF SALAD DRESSING YOU USE

Put your dressing in a little spray bottle so you use just a couple of spritzes.

stelladore

HOW TO QUICKLY SOFTEN BUTTER

Slice a stick of butter thinly and lay the slices on a plate. It will soften in minutes.

asildem

HOW TO REHEAT PIZZA

Heat up leftover pizza in a nonstick skillet on top of the stove over medium-low heat. This keeps the crust crispy. No more soggy microwave pizza.

AWade

HOW TO RIPEN AVOCADOS

To ripen avocados, put them in a paper bag with ripe apples. The apples give off a gas that causes the avocados to ripen quickly. When just right, keep them in the bottom of the fridge for two or three days if not eating at once.

Canopus

HOW TO SEED PEPPERS AND CHILES

When preparing chiles, always wear rubber gloves, especially if you wear contact lenses! Slice them in half and run a knife (away from you) down the chile; it should remove all seeds easily.

michelle_87

HOW TO SLICE AN ONION WITHOUT CRYING

This is a verified catering trade secret—just wetting the knife *or* the onion should do.

Abi1973

HOW TO STOP A SKIN FROM FORMING ON YOUR SAUCE OR GRAVY

My mother always puts plastic wrap directly on the surface of sauces and takes it off just before serving—it really works!

LucyD

HOW TO COAT COOKIE DOUGH BALLS IN SUGAR ALL IN ONE FELL SWOOP

Fill a plastic container with about 1 cup sugar, then drop in the cookie dough balls. Swirl them in the container with the lid on, and voila—all are thoroughly coated in sugar.

CeeVee

HOW TO GET A GORGEOUS FINISH ON A FROSTED CAKE

Once you've frosted the cake, no matter what type of icing, aim a blow dryer at it, turning as you go. The heat will melt the icing ever so slightly, giving you a beautifully uniform and smooth finish.

CeeVee

HOW TO IMPROVE ANY COOKIE RECIPE

Don't just soften the butter—melt it. Gooey to the max. Yum!

Tooke

HOW TO MAKE A QUICK CRUMBLE TOPPING

Grate butter (straight from fridge) on your cheese grater! It's amazing how quickly you can now rub it into your topping mixture!

bluma6914

HOW TO MAKE PERFECT COOKIES

For perfect and beautifully light pastry, I substitute self-rising flour for a quarter of the plain flour! Yes, I have had shrieks of "You can't do that," but trust me, it works. Even my mother-in-law liked the results, and she is a hard woman to please!

Kgirl

HOW TO MAKE SCONES, MUFFINS, AND OTHER BAKED GOODS COME OUT AS LIGHT AND FLUFFY AS THOSE IN BAKERIES

The key is in the handling. Scones can't be handled a lot or they become tough. Once you have made the dough, touch it as little as possible and roll out only as much as you need to.

With sponge cake, air is important. If a recipe wants you to mix butter and sugar, use an electric mixer to beat the butter by itself first, then add the sugar and beat again.

When a recipe asks you to add eggs, beat after adding each one to get more air in.

And try not to open the oven door a lot. The heat escapes and causes the batter to compress, making it dense.

wsslaoo

HOW TO STOP YOUR POTATOES FROM GROWING SHOOTS

Put an apple in with your potatoes to discourage the growth of shoots. Storing in a cool, dark place in a bag through which they can breath will keep them in good condition, too.

elizabethevelyn

HOW TO TELL IF OIL IS HOT ENOUGH FOR DEEP-FRYING

Drop in a single popcorn kernel at the beginning. When the kernel pops, the oil is between 350°F and 365°F— exactly the right temperature for deep-frying.

CeeVee

HOW TO MAKE GREEN TEA TASTE BETTER

Try a green tea blended with mint or lemon. Also, don't brew it for too long at first; you'll acquire the taste for a stronger cup as you become accustomed. Iced green tea might be more to your taste—though this is at its best in warm weather!

distractedhousewife

I always add a little honey to my green tea.

Redlady

Green tea is typically drunk in mountain countries such as Tibet and Nepal, at heights of 10,000 to 20,000 feet, water boils at 176°F or less (there is much less oxygen in the air at these heights and the air pressure is considerably lower). Green tea tastes delicious there, and is not at all bitter. It should not be made with boiling water like Indian tea, but infused at 176°F like herbal tea. Just take the kettle off a bit earlier—a few tries and you will find out exactly how much earlier. (Or use a thermometer!)

Canopus

HOW TO STEAM VEGETABLES WHEN YOU DON'T OWN A STEAMER

Bring a saucepan of water to a boil. Put your vegetables in a colander and place it on top. Cover with the saucepan lid—et voila!

Leilu

HOW TO TREAT MINOR BURNS

Keep an aloe vera plant in your kitchen so you can spread the sap on burns immediately.

Ruth

HOW TO GET FISH SMELL OFF YOUR HANDS

Rub your hands under running water with a stainless steel spoon or any stainless steel item. This works for garlic smells as well.

jadsia

HOW TO KEEP A MICROWAVE CLEAN

Always keep a clean sheet of paper towel on your microwave turntable. It will absorb anything that boils over and can be disposed of and replaced easily.

gillyano

HOW TO FIND THE END OF A ROLL OF PLASTIC WRAP

Gently rub an old (clean) toothbrush along the roll until you locate the edge. The bristles will help lift it up so you can grab it.

CeeVee

I fold over one corner whenever I pull out and cut plastic wrap. Then I just look for that corner the next time. I do this with packing tape as well.

Jillaroo95

HOW TO SEASON A CAST-IRON PAN

Cast-iron pans need to be seasoned to seal the metal before use. Wash and dry thoroughly, then coat with a thin layer of vegetable oil. Place on the top rack of the oven at 350°F for an hour. After an hour, turn off the oven and leave the pan to cool for several hours. Wipe with a paper towel. To maintain seasoning, wash only with clear water; never use soap or put it in the dishwasher.

DaisyMae

Eco

or Is my shoe closet a reflection of my carbon footprint?

The question is: Can you be bothered? Green is no longer the new black; however, the planet is still dying. This presents us with a conundrum. You used to get a lot of social kudos by being green, but it's no longer the fashionable obsession it once was. However, if we believe that global warming isn't a giant lunatic conspiracy, and even if other countries are racing to build thousands of Bond villain-esque filthy power plants, we still have to do what we can personally. Even those who espouse greenery still have a carbon footprint the size of Nantucket. So how are we going to get our big, eco-unfriendly feet into the slender pumps of the future?

HOW TO HELP THE ENVIRONMENT AND MAKE YOUR DAILY COMMUTE A LITTLE LESS DULL

Start a car pool. This may make your commute a little less stressful by providing time to catch up with a friend or discuss work issues before you get to the office. You may also benefit from preferential parking.

Tooke

HOW TO DISPOSE OF AN OLD BICYCLE AND MAKE A DIFFERENCE

Try contacting your local homeless shelter and see if the staff would like to give your old bicycle to one of the people they help.

Aaliyah

HOW TO DISPOSE OF OLD EYEGLASSES AND MAKE A DIFFERENCE

Donate your old glasses to a developing country and bring sight to the visually impaired. In some African countries, the price of a pair of glasses can exceed three months' wages. Check out lionsnwlerc.org.

BooBoo

HOW TO CUT DOWN ON YOUR ENERGY BILL

By adding draft guards to windows and doors, you can save money on your energy bill.

These are cheap to buy or make, and you'll make back their cost very quickly.

xthatscutex

HOW TO REDUCE WASTE PAPER

You can reuse most waste paper as scrap paper. Cut sheets down to smaller sizes and staple them together, ideal for leaving by the phone to scribble down messages.

LucyD

We waste loads of paper just by formatting documents with huge margins. I'm sure setting smaller margins, thus fitting more on the page, could save a forest.

FabulousFeminist

HOW TO RECYCLE MAGAZINES

Drop them off at the local hospital waiting area. We were recently at the hospital with our son for forty days and having something to read was very helpful to keep our minds off our worries.

sandrasimmons

HOW TO RECYCLE JUNK MAIL

Keep the envelopes for school use—lunch money, trip money, absence excuse notes, letters.

LJH

HOW TO REDUCE JUNK MAIL

A lot of junk mail comes with a postage-paid reply envelope. I stick the mail in the envelope (minus all personal details) and send it back. That way they have to pay the postage and gain no benefit. A bit mean, but maybe they'll get the message!

Isabelle

Unwanted mail can be curtailed by writing "Refused—return to sender" on the envelope. Mail it, and after a bit they will take your name off their database.

Canopus

HOW TO RECYCLE HOUSEHOLD ITEMS EASILY

Join freecycle.org. You won't believe the things they take: from a few bricks to door handles, paper, and more.

jadsia

HOW TO RECYCLE AND UPDATE YOUR WARDROBE

Arrange a clothes swap evening. Replace items you no longer wear and enjoy a fun night with friends.

Tooke

HOW TO MINIMIZE YOUR IMPACT ON THE ENVIRONMENT

Use a "gray water" system in your house that recycles shower, dish, laundry, and bathwater for jobs that don't need clean water, such as flushing the toilet. Approximately 65 percent of domestic water use is gray water, which could be reused. Obviously this does not include "black water," or sewage! It is a misconception that bathwater is bad for your plants: The dilution levels of normal soaps can actually aid absorption. Research online how to install a simple gray water system—or do it manually by reusing gray water in the garden.

Golda

I find that by doing my grocery shopping online, I buy only what I really need, as I don't get to see the bargains or other temptations that I would spot in the aisles of an actual store. This means that I waste a lot less food—I now throw away virtually nothing. Also, learn how to store your vegetables properly—e.g., put potatoes, onions, and bananas in bags designed to prolong their lives—so again, you are likely to throw away less. And get used to making meals out of leftovers. Try to use a delivery company with low-emission vans that make multiple deliveries in one journey, rather than driving to the store yourself.

Abi1973

Family

or Proceed with caution.

It is an immutable truth that no matter how crazy they drive you or how irritating and contrary they may be, no one else can criticize your family. As you complain bitterly about them, others can't even nod in agreement without a small surge of resentment emerging, which can build into a baseball bat of defensiveness. I would go so far as to say that it is dangerous to allow anyone to even be present if you're bitching about your family, because once your hissy fit is over that person may be tainted by association. A good tip to remind yourself how much you actually love your family is to imagine your criticism of your mother coming from someone else's lips—and see how you leap to her defense. But there is one thing friends can do that family can't—tell us off. If a friend tells me to pull myself together I think, "Fair enough," and get on with things sanguinely. If my mother does it, I immediately retreat to my standard five-year-old operating procedure and sulk. Sorry, Mum.

HOW TO ASK YOUR PARENTS TO LET YOU SHAVE
YOUR LEGS

When my daughter was younger and couldn't figure out how to talk to me about something, she would email me. That way, she didn't have to look me in the eye, and she could take her time over her wording. By the same token, I could take the time to consider my answer. When my daughter emailed me asking if she could shave her legs, she listed her reasons very logically and in a mature manner, and I said yes!

asildem

HOW TO NOT GET INVOLVED IN YOUR HUSBAND'S
FAMILY FIGHTS

Divorce him. Otherwise, you're a part of his family and you're going to be involved. You can get out of the initial or immediate fray by removing yourself physically, but the long-term situation is a concern of your husband's and, therefore, a concern of yours.

stelladore

HOW TO DEAL WITH AN INTERFERING MOTHER-IN-LAW

Can you direct her attention to something you don't care about but she does? Like, say, selecting the paint color for the interior of the garage. If you can manage to get her to "interfere" in ways that don't bother you (or bother you very little), then she'll have less time and energy for the things that really matter to you! One thing you really need to do is discuss the situation with your spouse and agree to a unified approach to what she does have a say in (e.g., the dessert for Easter dinner) and what she has to keep her nose out of (e.g., the number of, naming of, or rearing of the kids), and how to deal with her when she crosses the line (e.g., you correct minor infractions in real time; he promptly addresses the big ones).

DezG

HOW TO GET ALONG WITH YOUR MOTHER-IN-LAW

You'd be horrified if your partner were rude to *your* mother, so don't think you can get away with it, but there is a limit. Be charming and polite, buy gifts, etc., but realize that many women don't get along with their mothers-in-law, so you're not alone. Do everything you can and never bitch about the situation to your partner. You can calmly explain that this went wrong because of [whatever reason], but don't bitch. That's what your friends are for.

FabulousFeminist

HOW TO GET YOUR BOYFRIEND'S FAMILY TO ACCEPT AND LIKE YOU

I prefer that my son's girlfriends look clean and well groomed and not over the top in any way. A flattering pair of jeans is fine as long as the shoes, bag, etc. are in immaculate condition, and the hair and nails are newly done. I also like someone to help load the dishwasher and do other little chores without being asked—just get up and do it. What I do not like is someone who just sits there like a lemon and allows me to wait on her!

operatix

HOW TO GET YOUR ADULT SON TO ACCEPT YOUR NEW PARTNER WHEN YOU'RE A WIDOW

Ooh, this is a tough one. If your late husband had left you for someone else, your son would probably be furious with him and delighted that you'd met someone else to make you happy. However, speaking as someone who lost her beloved dad a couple of years ago, I have to admit that I'd struggle with anyone new in my mom's life. The best way you can approach this is to tell your son that you've been very lonely since his dad died and you don't want to be a burden to him or any siblings he may have. Whether it's true or not, tell him that your new partner will never mean as much to you as his dad did, and he'll never take his place, but he makes you happy and fills a great void in your life.

LindaCee

HOW TO MOVE BACK IN WITH YOUR PARENTS AFTER BEING INDEPENDENT

Remember that you are very blessed. You have people in your life who love you so much that they are willing to open their home to you and welcome you back. Not all parents would treat their adult children in this way. You are loved.

Do your own laundry, cook for them regularly. Bring cheap, cheery flowers home from your shopping trips and try not to slide back into the old way of doing things. You don't want to be treated as a child, so you must not behave like one. If they get a bit irritating at times, talk to them as though they were someone else's parents—it will help you stay firm and respectful and keep that teenage tone out of your voice. I'm thirty-eight and my mom can still bring out the sulky teenager in me!

Rosebudsmummy

HOW TO DEAL WITH BEING ESTRANGED FROM YOUR MOTHER OR FATHER

Call your parent and tell him or her you want to have a relationship based on polite, gracious, and courteous behavior. Don't rehash any of the problems you once had. This will make you the bigger person and the adult. Remember, they are your only parents, even if you think they are acting like kids. Rise above it all.

hillymo

HOW TO CELEBRATE MOTHER'S DAY ON A BUDGET

Give your mom a break from her daily chores: clean the house, do the washing, and make her some special meals, giving her time to relax and have the day off.

Gabrielle

HOW TO ENJOY MOTHER'S DAY WITHOUT YOUR MOM

If you know someone else who will be on her own, suggest getting together and having a day reminiscing about your mothers. This is a chance to enjoy the day and remember all the things your mom taught you.

Hayley

HOW TO FIND A PRESENT FOR A NEW MOM ON MOTHER'S DAY

New moms crave sleep, so the best present you can give her is a day off. Offer to look after the baby for a few hours, allowing her to relax and catch up on some much-needed beauty sleep.

Sarah

HOW TO MAKE YOUR MOM SEE THAT YOUR CRITICISMS OF HER WERE FAIR, EVEN THOUGH SHE SAYS THEY WERE DISRESPECTFUL

Your (hopefully constructive) criticism may be 100 percent accurate, but your delivery could still be disrespectful. Consider restaurant reviewers or theater critics—they may be right, but some of them are just mean! You should ask yourself why you feel compelled to criticize your parents in the first place. If your criticism is coming from a place of anger, just keep that thought to yourself (even if it's a fair observation). If it's something that is truly well meaning (e.g., a concern for her health), then make sure that you lead with the underlying concern, not the criticism.

DezG

HOW TO TELL YOUR MOTHER THAT YOU DON'T LIKE HER BOYFRIEND

Have a rational talk with your mother. Tell her that you don't like him and give her concrete reasons why this is so. Try your best to keep personal bias and emotion out of the conversation. If you sound calm and rational, you have a better chance of being listened to.

Jillaroo95

If you really feel it's important, do so, but be prepared for your mom to still see the man. She obviously likes something about him and just because you've registered a complaint doesn't mean she will stop seeing him.

stelladore

HOW TO TELL YOUR MOTHER THAT YOU ARE HOMOSEXUAL

Be honest with your mom, but please be prepared for a number of different reactions. Whatever happens, your mom will always love you, but she may be scared for your future, she may be disappointed that it's less likely that you'll have kids, she may be worried about her friends' reactions. All of those things are understandable to some degree, and you may need to be patient with her.

LindaCee

HOW TO DEAL WITH CANTANKEROUS PARENTS

If they are like this most of the time, you may need to learn to just let their moods wash over you. Not in a rude way—just smile slightly, nod, and don't let them get to you. You are your own person and entitled to your own opinions. Just don't force those opinions on them and hopefully they will not do the same to you. I'm at the stage where I can see my parents have differing views on things and some of the time I just have to count to ten, say nothing, and go with my own thoughts or ways of doing things. Once you do it a few times it's like second nature!

mimi18

HOW TO SOUND UPBEAT WHEN PHONING AN ILL MOTHER OR FATHER

The one thing that would mean more than anything is to let them know how much you love them. That's worth more than any amount of being upbeat. You could also tell them little amusing stories about things that happened to you that day. Let them into your life a bit and out of theirs, even for a few minutes.

Jillaroo95

This won't necessarily make you sound upbeat, but might be useful. Why not say you've been thinking about an episode in either their past or your mutual past and would like to be reminded of the details? It has to be a happy occasion.

That gives them something nice to talk about to each other and to you.

Cali

HOW TO TAKE YOUR ELDERLY PARENTS ON VACATION

For a start, remember that they're much slower at doing things than you are, so try not to be irritated by that. Arrange things so that you and the children have about twice as much to do as they have, which will take the same length of time.

Also try to remember that much as they love you all, they probably rather enjoy being by themselves sometimes, too.

Troops

Fitness

or Fit or fat, the choice is yours.

We all lie to ourselves about our bodies and how they work. We create fake equivalent systems where a walk to the bathroom equals a chocolate bar, or the accomplishment of some chore or other entitles us to eat lots. For this reason a considered attitude to fitness is essential. Decide to have a relationship with exercise, find the one you like, and if you're lucky you may become one of those people for whom it's as compelling and rewarding as sex. I've had brief glimmers, tiny windows into what it must be like to be one of those energetic fit people, but my attempts have been too inconsistent to be truly habit-forming. The truth is that the basics of fitness are extremely simple: move more. And good music helps. I genuinely and happily believe that I *am* Beyoncé as I stumble, inelegant as Barney, along the treadmill.

HOW TO REMEMBER TO DO PELVIC FLOOR EXERCISES

I do mine every time I'm on the phone to my boyfriend. He doesn't have a clue and I like to think I'm doing him a favor.

sunny2day2

HOW TO DO THE HULA

When you shake, bend your knees a little; you will see the difference. This is a great love handle squisher!

leilaniw

HOW TO MOTIVATE YOURSELF TO EXERCISE

Think of exercise like brushing your teeth—something that you need to do or it would be gross.

sandrasimmons

Think of a reason that makes you want to be in shape. I use the fact that I'm going to my best friend's wedding in Maui, where my ex-boyfriend and his new wife will be.

princessnata17

HOW TO BE MOTIVATED TO GO FOR A RUN IN THE EARLY MORNING

After you're fairly awake, allow yourself a choice. You can either go for the run, or you can stay at home and go back to sleep. The only catch is you have to stand in front of the mirror, look yourself in the eye, and say, "I am giving up on my fitness goal for today because I am too lazy," or something similar. A big trigger for me is to do the same thing, but in just my sports bra and shorts. That's a big reminder of what I'm trying to do.

miss_ali1984

HOW TO GET MOTIVATED TO START DIETING AND WORKING OUT

Sign up with a friend for a run for charity or, if you're a little more ambitious, how about a half-marathon? It really helps you get motivated, and you're doing good at the same time. Worked for me.

Kezz

HOW TO GET YOUR HUSBAND TO DIET AND EXERCISE

Find some healthy eating plans without even saying they're part of a diet. Your husband may start to enjoy the food.

Ally1310

HOW TO EASE THE PAIN OF SIT-UPS

Before you start doing sit-ups, lie on your back where you plan to do them, curl your knees up to your chest, and hold them. Then slowly release so your back is in the right position. This makes sure you're doing the sit-ups correctly and improves their effectiveness.

pandsy

HOW TO KNOW WHEN AND WHAT TO EAT WHEN EXERCISING

It depends on what exercise you are doing. If it is any type of weight training, eat some protein or drink it as a shake as soon as you finish the workout; then have a meal containing protein later on. If it's cardio, to avoid indigestion, wait until you feel that your body has returned to normal pace before eating.

pinkpantherjaime

HOW TO IMPROVE YOUR GOLF SWING/CLUB HEAD SPEED

If you want to develop a better swing and generate more speed with the club, you have a few options. You can start by having a professional club maker or repair person look at your clubs and advise whether the shaft flex is right for you.

Second, you can increase the width and length in your

backswing. This will generate more power and keep you on plane better.

Last, you can strengthen your lever system: your wrist hinge and your shoulder hinge. If you strengthen those muscles you will be better off.

behing01

HOW TO IMPROVE YOUR BREATHING WHEN
SWIMMING FREESTYLE

First, try to slow down your stroke. A common drill that swim teams use is to hold both arms in front, streamline position, kicking, then stroke with one arm, return it to the front, then stroke with the other—very slowly. As you do this, pay attention to when your elbow comes out of the water on the stroke arm; when the elbow is at it's highest, turn your head and start to breathe. As your hand comes forward and your fingers start to dive into the stroke, turn your head back into the pool. Also, be sure to exhale underwater so that you need less time to inhale out of the water.

DezG

HOW TO AVOID FOOT CRAMPS WHEN SWIMMING

Stretch before and after swimming (yes, stretch your feet!). Try heel raises, towel stretches, and flexing/relaxing toes, and make sure your diet has adequate potassium. If you are eating a high-protein diet or working out really hard, there's a chance your diet is low in calcium, magnesium, and potassium, all of which are necessary for proper muscle function. So add a good multivitamin or simply eat a banana a day.

DezG

HOW TO MAKE LAPS GO FASTER WHEN IN A POOL OR ON A TRACK

I bought a waterproof swimp3 music player. It has made swimming much more enjoyable.

meymez

HOW TO AVOID PICKING UP FOOT INFECTIONS AROUND SWIMMING POOLS

The lifeguards wear sandals, so why don't you? I keep a pair of clean flip-flops in my swim bag that I never wear outside. I put them on in the changing room and wear them out to the pool deck right until I get into the water. And I wear them in the showers, too; I don't take them off until I'm changing out of my bathing suit.

dewster

Friendship

*or Cling to the goodies, but be ruthless
in dumping the baddies.*

No matter what else is going on in our lives, we are in total control of whom we choose to be friends with. And we are defined by those choices. On my fortieth birthday I took stock and was immensely pleased and proud, not only of the friends I had chosen, but that they had allowed me to pick them. Whom have you chosen? Why? And what does that say about you? If they bring you down, dump 'em; but if they bring you joy, nurture them, hold them close, and never let them go.

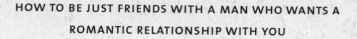

HOW TO BE JUST FRIENDS WITH A MAN WHO WANTS A ROMANTIC RELATIONSHIP WITH YOU

Start treating him like one of the girls. Don't ever dress up around him, just throw on sweatpants and tie your hair back. Let him see you with unwashed hair and a greasy face. Be casual about it. Give him advice (he'll stop feeling romantic about you straightaway), especially about the way he drives or the quickest route somewhere. Talk about your period pains. Ask him to go shopping with you. Call him up often for a chat. Invite him round to your place when lots of other people are there and be really friendly to everyone. Pat him on the shoulder. Tell everyone (in front of him) what a great pal he is. Ask him to drive one of your friends home. Don't tidy up your place when he comes round. In short—be super easy and comfortable, and the tension will go. Works like a charm.

ingridibus

Don't try—you'll only torture him. Let him out of your life so he can get over you, meet someone else, and come back to you as a neutral friend. Did reading that make your stomach turn? If so, reconsider whether that's all you want from him.

Abi1973

HOW TO RESPOND WHEN AN UNHAPPILY MARRIED
FRIEND EXPRESSES INTEREST IN YOU

Is he French? If so, this is normal behavior. If he is American, he needs to be told that you are not interested until there is a lot of clear blue water between him and his divorce.

Josa2

HOW TO TELL A GAY FRIEND THAT YOU DON'T LIKE HER IN
THAT WAY

You could paraphrase the quote from Jack Nicholson's character in *As Good as It Gets*—"You know, if that did it for me, I'd be the luckiest girl in the world."

Jillaroo95

WHAT TO DO WHEN FRIENDS HEAR YOU BITCHING
ABOUT THEM

Apologize. Tell them you've had a bad day and even the people you love most are getting on your nerves. Tell them it's about you and not them. If there are any real issues causing the bitching, leave them for another day.

Jillaroo95

HOW TO DEAL WITH A FRIEND WHO CONSTANTLY TEXTS AND USES HER PHONE IN YOUR COMPANY

Call her from your own phone when you are together and ask if this is the only way you can get to talk to her. If this doesn't work, then tell her firmly that you are there to talk to her, not to listen to her talking to other people, and would she be kind enough to turn off her phone when you are together.

Canopus

"Oh, wonderful!" you say, "You've remembered to bring your cell! I have some calls to make. I'm sure you won't mind."

catinthehat

HOW TO DIPLOMATICALLY GET A FRIEND TO BUY DRINKS FOR A CHANGE

Order drinks at the bar and just as they're being served go to the toilet, leaving your friend to pay for the drinks. Works every time.

jamesjoyce

HOW TO GIVE HONEST ANSWERS TO FRIENDS

Tact is key. Friendships are founded on honesty, but you must also be able to gauge correctly how much someone *needs* to know. "That's me, I'm just honest" is often shorthand for excusing rudeness and cruelty. Your friends must be able to trust you, but you should make a great effort not to hurt them in the name of your own honesty.

Abi1973

HOW TO MAKE FRIENDS WITH OTHER WOMEN WHEN YOU'RE NOT VERY GOOD AT IT

It's been my experience that the two main hallmarks of real friendship with other women are trust and emotional support. Can you be trusted not to go after another woman's boyfriend/fiancé/husband if you like him? Can you be counted on to offer a shoulder and/or assistance if your friend were having a tough time? Would you truly be happy for her if she got a promotion/became engaged/won an award?

Most women who are capable of being true friends with other women can say yes to all of these questions.

Jillaroo95

HOW TO REACT TO A FRIEND WHO KEEPS LETTING YOU DOWN

Why question her behavior? Look at your own. If she keeps letting you down, why do you believe she'll ever change? "The definition of *crazy* is doing the same thing over and over and expecting a different result." You cannot control the actions of others, but you can control your own.

DezG

HOW TO ADMIT WHEN YOU'RE WRONG

Keep asking yourself, "Would the earth stop spinning if I were wrong?" Do this until it sinks in. Oftentimes stubborn folks who feel they can't afford to be wrong received that indoctrination in their formative years. For whatever reason, they learned to put too much importance on not being wrong (and I'm speaking from personal experience here). But really, it's not that big a deal—most of the time—and you need to retrain yourself to truly believe that.

Jillaroo95

HOW TO ACT WHEN YOUR BEST FRIEND PUSHES YOU
AWAY JUST WHEN HER LIFE IS FALLING APART

She may not want to push you away; she may just be testing your friendship. Just be available when she's ready to need you again. Send her a card or note, perhaps something to make her smile, to let her know that you are still her friend and that you still care for her. Around the anniversary of my young son's death I tend to pull back from my friends, as if testing them to look after me for a while during a tricky time. We all get through it and back on track again after the difficult date. Your friend may be pushing you away if everything else is going wrong for her. She may feel she'll hurt you before you hurt her. Be gentle with her.

COLIYTYHE

HOW TO TELL SOMEONE YOU LOVE THAT YOU THINK THEY HAVE A DRINKING PROBLEM

You might start out by procuring a list of the warning signs of an alcoholic from your local alcoholism support center. Or you can find them online. Use this list as the basis for bringing up the subject. Emphasize that you are not judging but worried about someone you love.

Jillaroo95

HOW TO ENCOURAGE AN ANOREXIC GIRL TO EAT

The key thing is not to make an issue out of food or eating. Simply forcing the issue will have the opposite effect of what you want to achieve. Has the girl in question sought help? If not, then perhaps she's not ready to admit she has a problem. You should seek professional help from specialist support networks. The key thing is boosting her confidence (don't focus on her appearance but on her personality and other unrelated achievements).

Appleblossom1985

HOW TO WRITE A LETTER OF COMFORT TO SOMEONE WHO IS VERY ILL AND YOU DO NOT KNOW TOO WELL

It doesn't really matter what you write—the recipient will just be pleased that you have taken the trouble to write at all. I would start off by saying, "I know we don't know each other very well, but I just wanted to say how sorry I was to hear of your health problem" or something like that. Keep it short and to the point and offer practical help if you want, like dog walking, cooking, or whatever would be appropriate.

operatix

HOW TO HELP A FRIEND THROUGH CHEMOTHERAPY

Often people going through treatment for cancer say they can't concentrate on anything and can't read either. Audiobooks and CDs are a great gift. They can listen to them lying down without disturbing anyone and for a while forget about their illness. Try Bill Bryson's books—they're low-key and funny.

patsharp

Offer to drive her to appointments, take care of dinner for her (and family if needed), bring over a movie, send funny gifts or flowers, whatever your friend needs that you can provide.

stelladore

I'm afraid there may come a time when a little gentle bullying is required, too. My dad hated chemo so much that at one point, he talked about giving it up. This is where friends and families have to point out just how much the patient is loved and needed.

On a practical level, Dad always complained of having a horrible taste in his mouth, so a constant supply of jelly beans helped! Chemo can also cause very painful feet—something to do with the way it affects nerve endings—so something as simple as finding a pair of really comfy, thick-soled slippers can be a great help.

LindaCee

HOW TO BE NICE TO A FRIEND WHO'S GIVEN BIRTH

When you go and visit the new baby, be sure to take food. Ideally pop in at lunchtime and just take over the kitchen and prepare something nice while she dozes or nurses the baby. Then look after the baby while she eats.

euston74

I lent my friend all my DVDs of movies, TV shows, etc. Six weeks later, after she had a chance to have some time to herself, I visited again and she and her husband told me it was the *best* gift anyone had given them. They were able to watch them while she was breastfeeding, when they couldn't sleep in the middle of the night, etc. They borrowed them for about three months and really appreciated the thought.

kate42

HOW TO COMFORT SOMEONE WHO HAS JUST HAD A MISCARRIAGE

For her to recover it is crucial that she work out her emotions, talk openly about how she feels, and be allowed to grieve— bottling anything up will only make things worse, and those around her must remember that what she has gone through is both physically and emotionally traumatic. As a friend, you need to be on the lookout for any signs of depression (including less obvious ones like exhaustion, significant weight gain or loss, feelings of detachment, isolation, etc.) or guilt, and encourage her to seek professional help if these do arise. So be there for her, but focus on letting her do the talking/getting her to talk about how she feels. You can't make it better for her, so sometimes the best you can do is just listen.

Abi1973

I would suggest that you make a note of the baby's due date and on that day, or near to it, take flowers or send a card to let your friend know that you have not forgotten her lost baby. She will be feeling awful as the time of the baby's due date approaches and it really will be a comfort to know that she is remembered (I know, I've lost four babies).

COLIYTYHE

HOW TO REFUSE TO BABYSIT

A foolproof way to tactfully decline any sort of contact with a child is to say you're getting over a cold (you don't have to mention that the cold was actually last year). I've never yet met a parent who had the nerve to persist after that. If you're asked to babysit weeks in the future, say, "I have tentative plans for then; I'll let you know if they fall through."

asildem

HOW TO STOP A PREGNANT FRIEND FROM TALKING ONLY ABOUT HER PREGNANCY

You should listen to her. Being pregnant is a huge thing and is changing her life forever. She's probably very excited and a bit uncertain and needs her friends to support her. And if you think she talks about being pregnant a lot, wait until she has a child to care for and talk about!

stelladore

Tell her that all the hard work, devotion, and cost in raising a child culminate in the moment the child looks you in the face, smiles, and says those three magic little words: "I'm leaving home."

ladydigger

HOW TO HELP A FRIEND FIND THE STRENGTH TO LEAVE HER VIOLENT BOYFRIEND

I have a friend in the same situation. All you (and I) can do is be there to support her so she knows that when she's ready to leave him, she has a great support network around her. Let your friend know your door is always open, and let her talk as openly as she wants without passing judgment. You will be the first one she contacts when it does happen.

scottishchic

HOW TO TELL YOUR BEST FRIEND YOU THINK HER PARTNER IS CHEATING

Don't. There is no way you can come out of that situation un-damaged, and at the end of the day, it's none of your business. Be there for her if things blow up, but other than that, leave it.

LindaCee

Gifts

or I love it! (How could you?)

The greatest lie ever told by anyone in human history is "I don't want anything." These words have the toxicity of Three Mile Island. Keep away from them, do not listen to them, do not even entertain them, banish them—they are wrong. He or she doesn't mean it; it is a test. No matter what has been said to the contrary, everyone still experiences that childish crushing disappointment as they open a lame gift when everyone else is unwrapping what looks like gold, frankincense, or myrrh. That said, the presents that mean most are not the most expensive, but those that have the most thought behind them. Which is why you should buy them when you see them throughout the year, or at least make a list as they occur to you. Because as sure as eggs is eggs, on the eve of the recipient's birthday, tumbleweed will be billowing through the inspiration department of your head.

HOW TO BUY PRESENTS FOR A GEEK/NERD

Generally, there is one rule to remember—worthwhile technology costs money. If it's a cheap gadget, it's probably not worth having. Good-quality tech gadgetry costs in the hundreds of dollars—think Sony eBook or Amazon Kindle 2 rather than a USB Christmas tree. If that's out of your price range, fall back on the trusted geek staple of humorous and/or ironic T-shirts. A good website to visit is thinkgeek.com. Another is theonion.com. Also, anything with even an oblique reference to R2D2 on it is automatically cool. Happy Birthday/Christmas to us . . .

myfavoritesock

If you're completely stuck for ideas, ask for a gift list—what geek doesn't enjoy compiling lists?

siucra

HOW TO FIND THE RIGHT PRESENT FOR MY EIGHTY-FIVE-YEAR-OLD GRANDMOTHER

Get high-quality copies of her wedding photo/birth certificate and print pictures of her house, grandchildren, pets, favorite flowers, etc.—even photograph her engagement ring. Cut them out and then decoupage them onto a tray. Use many coats of varnish to make a tough surface. She'll use it every day and see all her nice memories on it.

patsharp

HOW TO HIDE PRESENTS FROM YOUR CHILDREN

If you have grandparents living nearby, hide them at their house. It's foolproof.

ashling

HOW TO KNOW WHAT SORT OF CAKE TO BAKE YOUR GUY ON HIS BIRTHDAY

There is much truth to the saying, "The way to a man's heart is through his stomach." The first year I was with my boyfriend (now husband) I did a "guy" cake. I bought a chocolate sponge base and iced it with the word *ass* in beautiful blue icing, surrounded with a ring of M&Ms. He nearly wet his pants laughing and still tells his friends about it five years later.

pussycatlover

I made my husband a two-tier meat pie instead of a birthday cake a couple of years back. Men are often savory rather than sweet critters and are easily amused by things out of scale.

distractedhousewife

WHAT TO BUY YOUR BOYFRIEND FOR HIS BIRTHDAY

Don't ask him what he wants. He doesn't want what he wants. What he *really* wants is to be delighted and surprised by your choice. Any woman who can get a man a favorite shirt always goes on a pedestal. A day out—driving fast cars, learning rock climbing, discovering falconry—may be expensive, but you could do it together. The autograph of his favorite sports star, made out to him. A really nice shaving brush. A poker lesson. Fifty feet of rope. An acre of rain forest. A voucher for some of your time to do with you as he wishes. Not socks.

Lemming

WHAT TO BUY A PREGNANT FRIEND

A pregnancy massage or a simple manicure/pedicure, and the offer to babysit during the appointment (if she has other children). It will be a treat that's all about her at a time when most people will be talking to her about babies.

Abi1973

WHAT TO BUY A PREGNANT FRIEND WHEN YOU'RE ON A BUDGET

There are lots of things you can do for pregnant women without spending any money, particularly if you are available during the day. Offer to paint or help decorate the nursery, do anything physical—e.g., do the grocery shopping, accompany her to doctor's appointments, be on hand to help after the baby is born, compile a scrapbook of baby tips (drawn from this book and friends with babies), do online research about things she needs (which are the best-rated strollers, cradles, car seats, etc.). Ask her what she would like you to do the most!

Abi1973

HOW TO GET THE GIFTS *YOU* WANT ON VALENTINE'S DAY, NOT WHAT HE WANTS YOU TO WEAR

My husband is on the autistic spectrum, so he doesn't really "get" hints—I have to tell him directly what I want, and remind him frequently of important dates. Once you get over the socially accepted idea that he should somehow just know these things, it is so much easier. I tell him what I want, and don't end up with rubbish. He knows what to get and doesn't panic. Everyone's happy, and we have a great day with no fights or disappointment. It's just a case of getting past the ridiculous idea society gives us that our partners are only romantic if they can mind-read!

Angiegw

HOW TO GIVE THE PERFECT WEDDING GIFT

If you know their honeymoon plans and interests, consider treating the couple to something indulgent during their honeymoon: a couple's massage, a hot-air balloon ride, a dinner at a posh restaurant, a day of scuba diving, tickets to a theater performance, etc. Have an announcement of the gift (or a gift certificate) sent to their hotel suite. Helping to create wonderful memories can be more meaningful than a vase or a set of towels (no matter how useful).

DezG

HOW TO WRAP PRESENTS FOR YOUNG CHILDREN

Buy big sheets of paper and either decorate them yourself or get the children to do it.

Boo

HOW TO WRITE A PERFECT THANK-YOU NOTE

Always send it sooner rather than later. If you're thanking someone for a present, say how kind the giver was to think of you and how lovely the gift is. Put a line in to say how the gift is being used. E.g., for slippers: "How cozy my feet are now!" Flowers: "They are opening up beautifully and the fragrance fills the room." If the gift was money, say how you plan to spend it or whether you are saving for something bigger.

COLIYTYHE

Hair

or If they can put a man on the moon, why can't they fix the frizzies?

air has a life and a mind of its own. You can do exactly the same thing, using exactly the same products in exactly the same order as you did yesterday, and yet, for some hellish reason, your hair refuses to play ball. Conversely, who hasn't experienced the phenomenon of Home Alone Sunday hair? You've done nothing to it at all and it looks better than it's ever looked, or is likely to look ever again. More important than clothes or makeup, your hair can influence your whole day. But if you're in any sort of relationship, resist the urge to spontaneously do anything drastic. Men really don't like it (no matter what they say) when women decide, for whatever reason, to change their hairstyle without warning. It may be your hair, and you may chose to ignore their views, but they love to be consulted.

HOW TO FIND A GOOD STYLIST FOR LONG HAIR

If you're brave enough, stop somebody in the street whose hair length, color, etc. is similar to yours and whose style you like and ask her which stylist she goes to. Anyone would be pleased and flattered to be approached in this way, and a personal recommendation is worth way more than an ad.

distractedhousewife

HOW TO GET GUM OUT OF YOUR HAIR

A very simple way to get gum out of hair is to drench it in olive oil. I promise, it works every time. Work it into the hair and gum and you can just slide the gum out.

Brianne

HOW TO GET HAIR DYE OFF YOUR SKIN

Hair spray or nail polish remover gets hair dye off, but be very careful to protect your eyes.

rencha

HOW TO GET STRONG HAIR

I am Pakistani and my mom always massaged either coconut or almond oil into my scalp and told me to keep it on all day or overnight. The trick is to wear a shower cap and place a towel over your pillow at night. When you're done, shampoo twice and condition very lightly.

chocolatenoor

HOW TO MAKE HAIR GROW FASTER

I massage my head for three minutes every single time I shampoo and condition my locks. I never cut it (sometimes the very ends get a teeny trim). Cutting hair regularly every few weeks may stop split ends but it makes your hair shorter. It certainly does not make it grow any faster. I also use homemade olive oil and beer hair masks. Mix it up, slather it on, wrap a hot damp towel around your head, watch a half hour of TV, and rinse out (thoroughly), and you too can have hair down to your hips like mine.

ladydigger

HOW TO GET RID OF THE GREASY RESIDUE THAT IS LEFT AFTER USING LICE LOTION

A vinegar rinse should take care of this. Lemon juice is also good and smells better, but vinegar rinses out more easily.

Buy a big bottle of malt vinegar and apply it carefully after shampooing, paying particular attention to the roots and scalp. Then rinse. A lot.

Rosebudsmummy

HOW TO GIVE MORE VOLUME TO YOUR HAIR

Backcomb! I swear by it, but don't go over the top. Just lift your hair up and backcomb bits underneath to give more volume and the impression of thicker hair. Spray some hair spray on when finished and voila, thick hair.

xXxLeannexXx

HOW TO KEEP SWIMMER'S HAIR CONDITIONED AND SHINY

If you're a regular swimmer and find it wreaks havoc on the condition of your hair, always wear a swimming cap, but before donning it, saturate your hair in conditioner. After a half-hour swim you can hit the shower and wash your hair in your usual way. Your hair will have benefited from an intensive "treatment" helped by the heat generated from your exercise—works for me!

antoinette

HOW TO MAKE CLIP-IN HAIR EXTENSIONS STAY IN

Backcomb your hair a little just in the place where the clips will sit; this gives them something to hold on to.

imi

HOW TO REMOVE HAIR-PRODUCT RESIDUE

Once a week, add a tablespoon of baking soda to your shampoo and conditioner. Your hair will feel so much cleaner!

chocolatenoor

HOW TO SPOT THE DIFFERENCE BETWEEN CONDITIONER AND SHAMPOO IN THE SHOWER IF YOU ARE NEAR-SIGHTED

Write a big C and a big S on the appropriate bottles using colored nail polish or a permanent marker.

PaulineGG

HOW TO STOP GETTING GREASY HAIR

Try washing it without scrubbing or rubbing your hair at all. Just use diluted shampoo, pour it over your head, and stroke it in gently. This will stop your scalp from being overstimulated and should ease the problem over time.

Bianca

HOW TO PREVENT HAIR FROM GOING WAVY IN HUMID WEATHER

My science teacher told me that if you use a wax product *very* sparingly on your hair, it acts as a barrier to the water of humidity.

kirstie123

HOW TO TAME FLYAWAY AND STATIC HAIR

All you need to do is spread a little of your lip gloss or lip balm over your hands and gently wipe them over the frizz.

Kimberley

Just spray a little hair spray on your brush before using.

patsharp

HOW TO TAME THICK AND FRIZZY HAIR

I have thick hair and use conditioner as you would a serum. It really controls my hair and keeps frizz at bay.

Redlady

HOW TO VOLUMIZE DULL, FLAT HAIR

To wake up tired, flat hair, spritz hair spray on your fingertips and massage through your roots—it works great!

AuntyV

Happiness

or Don't postpone it.

*H*appiness is sometimes thought of as a randomly bestowed blessing, which implies that it's out of your control. However (within certain parameters of moderately good health and a nonperilous standard of living), it is very much within your control. Millions of people work on their health and fitness—setting aside the time to do an hour of cardio three times a week—but most would feel self-indulgent to allocate an equal amount of time to actively pursuing happiness. Well, there are things you can do—simple, quick, efficient things such as making a list of things you are grateful for or doing something nice for someone else, which will tangibly boost your level of well-being. Who doesn't want that? So just get on with it.

"It takes as much energy to wish as it does to plan," said Eleanor Roosevelt. Start making plans for something you've only dreamed about so far.

abi1973

Pay for the person behind you in the line: at the newsstand, at the café, at the supermarket—whatever you can easily afford.

Troops

Before bed, consider what you've done that you're proud of today and what you will do to be proud of tomorrow.

Gretchen

Bake something and take it to the office to share with colleagues. There's nothing like homemade yummies to spread happiness at work.

Esme

Smile. At everyone, everywhere. *All day*. Particularly strangers. Even if they look at you strangely.

libbyuk2003

Think of a compliment you would like to receive and act in a way that deserves it.

Emerald

I follow Mma Ramotswe's advice on the subject of happiness. She is quite clear on this; she says that the surest way to be happy is to cause happiness in others and then to enjoy it oneself. I think she is right.

Alexander McCall Smith

I sometimes need to remind myself that my happiest times are when things are pretty simple: having takeout on the kitchen table with family and friends, for example (with a good bottle of wine). The message is, I think, don't overcomplicate, as often you remember the mood, not the detail. Oh, and being somewhere with good BlackBerry coverage!

Anya Hindmarch

Do not expect to be happy, then it might sneak up on you.

Bel Mooney

Enjoy every minute.

Brent Hoberman

My tip for happiness is to "believe the best in everyone." It's amazing, if you live by this mantra, how rarely you are disappointed, and it makes the world seem a much happier place.

Charles Dunstone

Cuddle more. Tickle more. Sleep more.

Claudia Winkleman

Swim at dawn on an empty Cornish beach.

David Cameron, Prime Minister of Great Britain

Wear a fabulous smile and great jewelry and know that you are totally and utterly in control!

Donatella Versace

There's a Chinese proverb: "Those the Gods hate, they satisfy their ambitions." I find that comforting because it implies that ultimately happiness is in the striving, not the succeeding.

Jemima Khan

Nature is the one thing that sustains me. I think people don't put their feet enough on the earth. As Wordsworth said, "Nature never did betray the heart that loved her." And there's that wonderful saying by Sacheverell Sitwell: "The birds sing on the trees for rich and poor." That, and giggling with my husband in bed in the morning, and a large drink in the evening.

Jilly Cooper

Things that make me happy . . . a glass of Jack Daniel's at the end of a crazy week . . . landing a pontoon start and wake-boarding behind a speedboat. A good massage from someone with firm hands and sitting on a beach as the sun goes down, watching my kids play in the sea. Wish I was enjoying one of those right now!

Jo Whiley

Work as if the money doesn't matter. Love as if you have never been broken-hearted. And dance as if no one is watching.

P.S. Also, don't feel bad about pinching other people's

ideas: I was given this advice by my dancing partner, Kristina Rihanoff.

John Sergeant

Read your kids a bedtime story.

Viscount Rothermere

In the words of Cole Porter, "Make someone happy." Happiness is also Twitter, family (sometimes!), sleep, and a tidy house.

Kirstie Allsop

Create something.

Luke Johnson

Love and be loved.

Martha Lane Fox

Eat peanut butter and jam on toast.

Nick Clegg, Deputy Prime Minister of Great Britain

Eat, drink, and nap.

Nick Jones

Don't take yourself too seriously.

Niklas Zennstrom

As Joseph Campbell said, "Follow your bliss."

Peter Gabriel

Being with my sons.
Finishing a book.
Starting a book.
Being in the middle of a book.
Jameson's on the rocks.
Vivian Blaine singing "A Person Could Develop a Cold"
    from the movie Guys and Dolls.
The Uffizi Museum.
The song "Bombay Meri Jaan."
The company of friends.
Watching Roger Federer play tennis.
Kindness.
New York City.
Bombay.

Salman Rushdie

Happiness is having a husband who makes you laugh.

Sue Lawley

Give your time to the people who matter most to you and re-member who you are irreplaceable to.

Tessa Jowell

How to be happy is for me very easy! The biggest pleasure any-one can give anyone is cooking them a delicious home-cooked meal; it always brings a smile to anyone's face.

Tom Aikens

Think of yourself in the future, lying on your deathbed. You look back on your life and think:

1. Have I made the most of my life on this earth?
2. Did I do everything I could to make sure I was happy? Big things and little things?
3. Did I make other people happy?

Then snap back into the present and be so very grateful you are not on your deathbed yet, and realize that we really *do* get only *one* life, which is very precious, so don't waste it being unhappy—make every day count and start by deciding now, at this very minute, that you are going to be *happy* goddammit, regardless of what life throws at you. In the end we will all end up the same way—life is for living, so start living it *now*!

willkat

A life coach gave me this tip: When I wake up, I think to myself that today will be a great day, and I am going to stay happy all day and just have fun. I didn't really believe her at the time, but I tried it and it really does work.

laurenfitz

Try avoiding people who are often miserable and depressed. Keep with the smilers and enthusiasts. That doesn't mean that you should ditch your best friend when her man dumps her and she genuinely needs a shoulder to cry on, it just means try to stay away from the moaners until your spirits lift.

MinErvaBytes

1. Be impeccable with your word, meaning tell the truth and don't gossip.
2. Don't take anything personally. Everything anyone says, even if they say it about you, is about them, not about you.
3. Don't make assumptions.
4. Always do your best.

    asildem

Make a list of things you never complain about. It focuses your mind on all the things you are grateful for. They say, "Change your attitude and you change the world." It works!

    Bridget

Make a real effort in planning and doing those things that will make you feel better about yourself and happier, such as a charitable act, doing something nice for a friend, a fun outing, challenging yourself with a new hobby, etc. So many people make plans for other aspects of their lives but think that happy moments should just occur by happenstance. There's no reason why you can't do something concrete and actually form plans to make your life generally more happy.

    Jillaroo95

Remember, no matter how much you may feel that it's not the case, *you* (and no one else) are responsible for your own happiness. If you are not happy, work out what the problem is, and solve it.

    Leilu

Health

or Remember those magic words, "OK, you better not go to school today"? Now that I'm grown up, I sometimes say them to myself.

There is little more riveting than your own health and little less riveting than the health of others. (Just like dreams, really.) Even the tiniest manifestation of ill health can be absorbing and fascinating in oneself, and yet nothing gets old quicker than someone else going on about their hay fever or ingrown toenail. Only when health issues become serious do things really get interesting. A great friend of mine who is a breast cancer survivor reminds me that there is nothing more important than perspective when she says, "Some people have stage 4, so how lucky am I?" And when she laughs, "I didn't have to take out the garbage for ages!" she also happily demonstrates that black humor is simply human and helps to make illness bearable.

HOW TO CURE A SORE THROAT WITH NATURAL INGREDIENTS OR RESOURCES

Chile is a natural antiseptic and takes down swelling, strange as it may seem. A good hot curry, preferably made with fresh chiles, will eliminate a sore throat immediately.

Canopus

HOW TO PREVENT CATCHING THE COMMON COLD

Wear gloves on all public transportation (or wash your hands as soon as you arrive), and always use your elbow, never your hands, to open the doors of public lavatories.

Canopus

HOW TO DEAL WITH CYSTITIS

When I had agonizing pain, peeing every three minutes, the best remedy was to sit in a hot bath of water for an hour or two and just pee in the water. It took a lot of the sting away while I waited for the antibiotics to kick in. I know it sounds gross, but try it.

marilynpanto

HOW TO GET RID OF BLOATING

Try fennel tea. It's also great for treating colic.

venus01

HOW TO GET RID OF EMBARRASSING GAS

Peppermint tea! Works wonders! Drink it regularly throughout the day (perhaps substitute it for a couple of cups of regular tea or coffee) or after you've had a big meal.

Kwilky

HOW TO GET RID OF TRAPPED WIND THAT'S CAUSING A STOMACHACHE

Even if it's the last thing you feel like, some form of physical activity will help get things moving.

If you're in pain or feel bloated, I recommend lying on your back, knees bent, with the soles of your feet on the floor. Keeping your trunk stable, lower both knees together toward your left side until they touch the floor. Let them rest there for a few seconds. Repeat on your right side. Keep repeating this move for as long as you like; the twisting motion gradually helps relieve the built-up tension. Just make sure you have some privacy as it will likely make you a bit windy afterward!

For less severe pain, I find just going for a stroll relieves the tightness.

sunny2day2

HOW TO GET MORE VEGETABLES INTO YOUR DIET WHEN (A) YOU DON'T EAT ANY AT THE MOMENT AND (B) YOU REALLY DON'T LIKE THEM

Pizza! Buy a thin-crust plain tomato and mozzarella pizza and before you put it in the oven, try "decorating" it with combinations of vegetables. Ones that work particularly well are mushrooms, corn, onions, peppers, artichoke, small broccoli florets, asparagus, olives, spinach, shredded carrot . . . or anything else you fancy experimenting with. You can get some great flavors this way, and it's well-balanced but still feels naughty and enjoyable.

sunny2day2

HOW TO GET RID OF A MOUTH ULCER

This sounds weird, but it really does work. My mom taught me this one. Take some powdered (*not* granulated) sugar and pack it around the ulcer. Do this over one evening, adding sugar as needed. Apparently, it helps the membrane in that area seal and heal itself more quickly. Since I learned this, I can get rid of a mouth ulcer in a couple of days rather than wait a couple of weeks for it to go away on its own.

Jillaroo95

HOW TO PREPARE FOR A PAP SMEAR

If you wear a skirt, you can hitch it up rather than take it off—
this can make you feel less exposed. Plus afterward, when you
hop off the table, you feel dignified immediately instead of
having to find underwear and pants first.

Rosebudsmummy

HOW TO STOP COMPULSIVE HAIR PULLING

I used to pull at my hair all the time when I was embarrassed
or flustered. I found that fixating on another silly thing to do
instead of pulling at my hair helped me break the habit. For
instance, I would tap my fingers or tug on my pocket. Eventually the habit grew less compelling and I was able to stop
doing things compulsively altogether.

MeVsEveryone

HOW TO QUIET RESTLESS LEGS

I have had restless legs, and now one of my arms, since I was
a teenager. I find that if I take magnesium every day, it amazingly disappears after about ten days and comes back only if I
stop taking it.

Ermentrude

I find that taking zinc in the morning can help.

gillmatt

HOW TO SOOTHE A JELLYFISH STING

When I was stung by multiple baby jellyfish in Mexico, the locals told me to put sand from the beach on the places I'd been stung. It worked surprisingly well, especially since I didn't have any vinegar or burn cream, and who wants someone peeing on you?

princessnata17

HOW TO AVOID MOSQUITO BITES WHILE SLEEPING

Buy some fresh and smelly basil, and put it next to your bed.

abiusoft

HOW TO STOP A MOSQUITO BITE FROM ITCHING

Rub a wet bar of soap all over the bite area and leave it to dry—it'll stop the itching!

Yvette

Several things work: Apply clear nail polish (yes, it's true!); mix baking soda and water and smooth it on with your fingertips;

rub banana peel on the area or rub the bite gently with a piece of lemon.

Failing that, you can always go with calamine lotion.

WelshWonder

HOW TO HEAL POSTBIRTH STITCHES FAST

Wheat germ oil is even better than vitamin E oil for healing scars. You can find capsules at health stores; just break them open and apply the oil two or three times a day. It smells a little funny, but is well worth it.

daniegenie

HOW TO DEAL WITH COLD SORES

Use licorice balm on a daily basis and you won't get any more cold sores.

Redlady

HOW TO STOP YOURSELF FROM DRINKING THE WHOLE BOTTLE OF WINE WHEN YOU HAVE ONE OR TWO GLASSES BUT THE REST KEEPS LOOKING AT YOU

Put the cork back in and put the bottle out of sight, then go and brush your teeth—I guarantee you won't fancy the wine then!

milli74

HOW TO DRINK ON A NIGHT OUT WITHOUT GETTING TOO WASTED

My grandmother had a great idea. She would have one gin and tonic at the beginning of the night, and when anyone asked her if she wanted another she would say that her current one was a bit strong—could she just have it topped off with tonic. She repeated this throughout the evening and everyone always saw her with a full glass, but actually she had only one shot all evening.

Angiegw

HOW TO SURVIVE HAY FEVER—A CURE FOR RUNNY ITCHY EYES AND RUNNY NOSE

Honey. Try to buy your local honey; take a spoonful every day and it will ease your symptoms. Ideally you should start this before the hay fever season begins.

mophead

I have endured awful hay fever for years and what I've found recently that works the best is the simplest thing. Religiously have a shower or bath before you go to bed and leave the clothes you've been wearing outside your room (preferably wash them). Throughout the day you can pick up pollen on your skin, clothes, and hair; if you wash it off you can avoid

the nighttime sneezing fits and hopefully wake up feeling re-
freshed and not puffy-eyed!

Gemrose

HOW TO GET TO SLEEP WHEN YOU FIND IT IMPOSSIBLE
AND HAVE TRIED EVERY TRICK IN THE BOOK

Eating a banana during the hour before bedtime has completely cured my husband, who was an insomniac for years.

Canopus

HOW TO DEAL WITH NIGHT SWEATS

My doctor told me to take soy capsules or eat more things with
soy (edamame, soy milk, etc.) to deal with night sweats and
hot flashes specifically. He also advised vitamins E and D as
well as calcium. It's a bit of a pain to remember to take all of
those, but so far it's really paying off.

stelladore

HOW TO GENTLY REMOVE THE STICKY MARKS LEFT BY
HORMONE REPLACEMENT THERAPY PATCHES

WD-40 removes anything sticky.

patsharp

HOW TO PREPARE FOR YOUR PERIOD AND COPE WITH EXHAUSTION AND CRAMPING

Everything I've read about easing period symptoms suggests taking evening primrose oil. Also, for some reason, I find taking iron supplements the week before and during my period helps. Another sickening but useful suggestion is light exercise. Hate it, but it does bring relief.

gduffy85

HOW TO REMEMBER TO TAKE YOUR BIRTH CONTROL PILL EVERY DAY

If you're working, you normally get up at the same time every day. The first thing most of us do when we wake up is pee. Keep your pill in the bathroom close by so you can spot it while you're peeing; the minute you're done, take your pill.

I have been doing this for about ten years now and have never forgotten to take the pill or gotten pregnant.

Delsi

HOW TO BREASTFEED

Before you get into position, make sure you have a glass of water, a large bag of your favorite chocolates, the TV remote, and your phone within easy reach as you could be there for hours, and it's hard to move once you've started.

Esme

HOW TO CURE CONSTIPATION DURING PREGNANCY

Eat a small package of prunes and buy packs of them to keep in your purse—a safe snack when you're pregnant because it is just dried fruit.

Bubblicious

HOW TO DEAL WITH WATER RETENTION IN PREGNANCY

Eating celery helps as well as drinking more water.

pinkpantherjaime

HOW TO GET YOUR PARTNER TO UNDERSTAND THE IRRATIONAL, OVERSENSITIVE BEHAVIOR THAT IS COMMONPLACE IN PREGNANCY

I think the best way to make him understand is to sit down together when you're *not* feeling like a crazy person and have a laugh about it. Explain to him that the way you are feeling drives you mad, too, but it's short term (you hope!) and his relatively sane partner will be back in the house at some point. Emphasize that any snappishness is not directly aimed at him—he's just the nearest target. Also, try to explain how fat and unattractive you feel right now. If it provokes a few more compliments and hugs, all the better.

TizzysMum

HOW TO STOP MORNING SICKNESS

Eat little and often. I found that starchy foods worked best for me, especially those that take a long time to digest like oatmeal (I used to have a bowlful before going to bed at night, as I found I felt less sick when I woke). Also, ginger is an old remedy—ginger cookies, ginger beer, even sucking on a cube of crystallized ginger will help.

chickenlady

HOW TO INCONSPICUOUSLY REFUSE ALCOHOL AT A STAFF CHRISTMAS PARTY WHEN TWO MONTHS PREGNANT

Be the driver, which means you can't drink—problem solved!

DOZIGGY

HOW TO DEAL WITH PSORIASIS

Chickweed worked wonders for my sister! You can infuse the herb or buy it in a cream form.

andrea39

HOW TO TREAT SUNBURN

Soak a towel or facecloth in white vinegar diluted with a little cold water, then lay it on the sunburn. It will take the burn out of your skin. I promise this works.

Redlady

Calamine lotion works well, especially if you can keep it in a fridge. And it's really cheap. I've traveled all over Asia and have found it in every country.

Caterina31

Rub plain yogurt on the area, leave it to set for half an hour, then wash off. This should make it less red and painful.

ameliabelia

HOW TO GET RID OF WARTS

I had a wart for about ten years and none of the medications available worked. I then read about using banana skin. I was dubious, but I tried it and it was absolutely amazing; it cleared up my wart in about a month. Cut a square of banana skin large enough to cover the wart, place the fleshy side against the wart, and keep in place with a normal bandage. You'll notice a difference after twenty-four hours. Change every evening. I swear it works; it's amazing!

Georgie137

HOW TO EAT WHATEVER YOU WANT ON A DIET

Eat only until you are full. Most people overeat, which causes weight gain. If you eat more slowly and put down your fork between each bite, you'll be more aware of your body and when you're full. And, of course, you absolutely have to exercise.

stelladore

HOW TO FEEL FULL FOR LONGER

Have a big glass of water before you eat.

xxHazeLxx

HOW TO FIND CALORIE-FREE CANDY

Stick some grapes in the freezer! They taste sweet and have hardly any calories. Munch a few and you get one of your five a day. Very tasty, too.

minx26

HOW TO STOP CRAVINGS WHEN ON A DIET

Keeping busy is key: Your mind must be fully occupied and it helps if your body is, too, so get deep into something you love that's at least marginally active (telling you to go to the gym would just be cruel). Ideally get away from the kitchen as well. So going shopping is good (who ever *needs* to stop for cake when they're shopping?); watching TV and puttering around the house is bad! If at work with time to spare, throw yourself into tidying your desk, sorting your in-box, or making a free interactive food log on a site like fitday.com to horrify yourself with how many calories are contained in the things you're craving.

Abi1973

HOW TO IMPROVE WILLPOWER WHEN ON A DIET

A picture is worth a thousand words. Take a photo of yourself—from behind—and keep it handy. Every time you are tempted to eat that plate of chips, look at that picture.

Jillaroo95

HOW TO LOSE WEIGHT

It's so easy to kid yourself that you don't eat that much and just looking at a doughnut makes you put on weight, but we all know that's not true. Keep a food diary (be honest) of what you eat—you'll be amazed how much. I use the "stop eating before you're full" method and try not to snack too often. Always choose healthy food over junk and your body will respond naturally. It's great being slim, and anyone who says otherwise is a great big fibber!

Ali161

HOW TO MOTIVATE MY BOYFRIEND TO LOSE WEIGHT

Why don't you suggest that you two have a competition to see who can get the fittest by Christmas/Easter/summer/whenever? Think of a suitably saucy prize for the winner . . .

Troops

HOW TO SPEED UP YOUR METABOLISM

Exercising and taking cold showers will speed up your metabolism.

Tallulah

The Holidays

or Brace yourself...

The holidays are really two things: the special days themselves, which are full of spiritual significance, love, family, and tidings of comfort and joy, and the entertaining aspect, which is a logistic act of preparation on a par with the D-day landings. Thus, make provision early (buy wrapping paper and decorations in the January sales, save for gifts throughout the year, and cook and freeze whatever you can ahead of time), and you will be able to enjoy the true loving spirit of the holidays, without a grimace born of exhaustion, resentment, and too much sherry.

HOW TO AVOID WEIGHT GAIN OVER ANY HOLIDAY

Small helpings! I put everything on my plate, just in tiny, tiny amounts.

lynzbear21

HOW TO BUY GIFTS ON A BUDGET

Send a group letter to the adults on your gift list and tell them that gift buying is getting out of hand and suggest you all take a break this year or impose a top limit of say $20 per gift between you. Most people will find the proposal a great relief.

jennywd

You could make candies and cookies and wrap them in colored cellophane. If you can crochet or knit, make some scarves, or bottle some homemade chutney. Another good idea is to buy fabric remnants and sew travel makeup bags for the women and toiletry bags for the men.

Jillaroo95

One Christmas when I had no money, I gave my family vouchers of my time. To my brother I gave a voucher for washing his car and to my father, one for cooking a three-course dinner. I made the vouchers up on nice cards, which I decorated.

pussycatlover

HOW TO AVOID GOING BROKE AT THE HOLIDAYS

Hit the January sales. You can pick up loads of holiday stuff at a fraction of the price. I try to buy all of my wrapping paper, cards, and decorations and then store them away.

sophie08

Open a savings account and each month put in a set amount. This way you'll have funds for gifts and entertaining, and saving small amounts won't hurt so much along the way.

Emu80

HOW TO PREPARE A BUDGET FOR THE HOLIDAYS

Make menu, gift, trips, and expenses lists. Total their cost, divide by twelve, and try to put away that amount each month.

ashling

HOW TO TELL MY FRIENDS I DON'T HAVE MONEY TO SPEND ON THEM THIS CHRISTMAS

I buy all my gifts at thrift shops and get really outlandish things for my friends. Nothing over $10 is permitted. They love the gifts! My list last year included a jigsaw of the highway, a CD of Mongolian nose-flute music, and one of those dolls with the bell-shaped skirt to fit over a spare toilet roll. They love them and remember exactly what I buy them each year (probably with horror).

ladydigger

HOW TO MAKE YOUR HOUSE SMELL LIKE A CHRISTMAS TREE

I'm an essential-oils fan and at Christmas use frankincense or pine and cinnamon oil in an oil burner for a lovely festive smell.

ashling

HOW TO SURVIVE THE HOLIDAYS

Start creating your own traditions based on things that make you happy.

Jillaroo95

Starting a month in advance, try to do/organize/plan one thing each day, however small or large. It could be as simple as deciding which crackers you want or as (potentially) complex as working out your cooking timetable. This may help spread the load and allow you to feel more in control!

Labink

HOW TO SURVIVE THE DAY ITSELF

Prepare in advance. Peel vegetables etc. the night before.
  Use prepared foods. Don't try anything new!
Follow a rough timetable.
Wash up as you go along. Bribe the children and husband
  to lend a hand.
Be moderate where food and alcohol are concerned; a
  little of what you fancy does you good!
Be moderate also in your expectations of gifts, help, and
  gratitude.
Try self-hypnosis and go on automatic pilot mode.
Dress up but wear comfortable shoes!
Record TV shows you're desperate to watch and don't
  argue when others want to watch something different.
Smile! Whatever happens, pretend it doesn't matter; you
  meant it to happen!
Say "thank you" for another holiday in good company.
  Millions of people aren't so fortunate.

  Eirlys

HOW TO ARRANGE TREE LIGHTS PERFECTLY

First plug them in and turn them on to make sure they're still
working. Then arrange them on the tree before you put on any
other decorations.

  AnitaL

HOW TO PREVENT CATS FROM DESTROYING YOUR DECORATIONS

Have a spray bottle filled with water nearby at all times and spritz the cats with water when they start getting out of line.

FabulousFeminist

Home

or One of the great questions of philosophy: Where do all the socks go?

It's amazing that something as prosaic as laundry could be responsible for one of the greatest supernatural phenomena of our time. The missing sock has inspired poems, polemics, and desperate pleas to Saint Anthony. The extraordinary thing is that you only find lone socks in your drawer or the dryer, rather than skulking around the house as they surely must be. I suspect that they actually abscond in tribes, but occasionally one gets left behind, perhaps as a ruse to divert the hapless owner into searching for just its mate, rather than the whole happy band who have made a successful bid for freedom. Colluding with the naughty socks is the more tiresome colored item that worms its way into your whites wash. I suspect that they cling to the roof of the washing machine like an old-fashioned crook clinging to the underside of a train, just waiting for the perfect moment to drop silently into your previously pristine life.

HOW TO SWAT A FLY

A really easy way to swat a fly is to wait until it comes to rest on something. Get a rolled-up magazine (or your weapon of choice) and come at it from the front—imagine hitting it on the nose. I used to creep up behind them (forgetting about their compound eyes) or come down flat, but since I heard that they can only take off "forward," thus virtually flying into the swat, my success rate has improved dramatically.

Tooke

HOW TO DETER WASPS

Try hanging a large paper bag, tied at the top and suspended on a string, from a tree or the overhang on your porch. Wasps are very territorial and will not bother you if they think that there is a larger and stronger colony nearby.

agnes123

HOW TO IMPROVISE WHEN YOU NEED A LOW TABLE OR WORK SURFACE

Most ironing boards have an adjustable height so, when you are short on space, use yours as a table! I sit on the end of my bed and lower mine until it is the right height—good when I need to get out my sewing machine.

Judi

HOW TO KEEP STEEL WOOL RUST FREE

After you've used the steel wool, pop it in a bag in the freezer. It won't rust and you'll be able to reuse it many times.

genw

HOW TO KEEP A SHAVING CREAM CAN FROM RUSTING AND STAINING THE BATHROOM TILES

Before first use, coat the bottom of the shaving cream can with clear nail polish. This stops moisture from reaching the metal, and therefore stops rust from forming.

CeeVee

HOW TO OPEN A TIGHT SCREW-TOP LID OR JAR

Run the lid but not the jar under hot water—metal expands when heated and allows the jar to open easily. Then use a dish towel to turn the lid.

star

HOW TO CLEAN A VERY DUSTY ROOM

Use a damp cloth first—the dust will just fly around if you use a dry cloth. Then use a normal polish and duster.

Shawfire

HOW TO CLEAN BURNT POTS

I pour a can of Coke into the pan and boil it. If that fails, fill the pan with water, add a dishwasher tablet, and leave it to dissolve—for a while—that seems to work!

LucyD

HOW TO CLEAN COPPER PANS NATURALLY

Use ketchup! Spread it on, let it sit, then wash it off. This works amazingly well on my copper-bottomed pans, which can get really nasty on an electric stove.

jcull

HOW TO CLEAN TOILET BRUSHES

I found that leaving the toilet brush in the toilet bowl with detergent while I clean the rest of the bathroom cleans it.

LucyD

HOW TO CLEAN LIMESTONE COUNTERTOPS

The porosity makes limestone counters prone to staining, even if you've had them sealed.

Clean with a mild dishwashing soap solution.

Do not use abrasive cleaners or ones containing lemon, vinegar, or other acids—they will dull the surface.

beksb

HOW TO CLEAN PEWTER

Try rubbing it with a cabbage leaf. Sounds mad, but it works.

corkychum

HOW TO CLEAN WATER STAINS FROM MARBLE TOPS

Try white wine vinegar.

Myspandex

HOW TO CLEAN WINDOWS

Microfiber cloths straight out of the washing machine! You simply wipe over your windows (in seconds) and fling back in the washer—no streaks either.

Kate12

HOW TO FADE WATERMARKS ON ANTIQUE WOOD

Put 2 tablespoons of table salt in a small bowl; then stir with enough olive oil to make a paste. Using a cotton cloth, rub some of the paste in a circular motion on the water stain. The salt acts as an irritant, loosening the stain and dirt; at the same time the oil lubricates the wood. Should work beautifully.

marjorieUSA

HOW TO FIND THE JOY IN HOUSEWORK

I make it bearable by putting on some energetic music and dancing around and singing along as I do it. Think of it as a workout.

beksb

HOW TO GET RID OF COBWEBS ON HIGH CEILINGS

Tape a feather duster to a broom. Job done with no climbing!

bekki007

HOW TO GET RID OF FISH ODORS IN THE HOUSE

Put a bowl of vinegar in the oven and set on a medium heat to eradicate the smell of fish.

Abi1973

HOW TO GET RID OF A MUSTY ODOR IN DRESSER DRAWERS MADE OF PLYWOOD

Sprinkle bicarbonate of soda in the drawers, rub it in, leave it to work, and then vacuum it out.

Mazcom

HOW TO GET THE SMELL OF BABY VOMIT FROM CAR UPHOLSTERY

Sprinkle some bicarbonate of soda over the stain and gently rub it in; it will remove the smell completely. It is inexpensive and works!

indogirl

HOW TO KEEP SILVER FROM TARNISHING

Keep a large piece of blackboard chalk with the silver—preferably in a reasonably airtight container. It works by wicking away the moisture that would otherwise tarnish the silver. Amazing.

Pilar

HOW TO KEEP THE TOILET CLEAN

Once a week drop a denture cleaner tablet into the toilet and leave overnight.

Redlady

HOW TO KEEP YOUR KITCHEN SPONGES FROM
BREEDING BACTERIA

Put them in the microwave for a minute; this kills off the nasties.

daisyfay

HOW TO REMOVE CANDLE WAX FROM A PAINTED WALL

Put three or four ice cubes in a plastic bag and hold the bag against the wall for about ninety seconds. Then scrape downward on the wax with an old credit card; it should pop right off.

gduffy85

HOW TO REMOVE HAIR SPRAY FROM THE
BATHROOM FLOOR

Rubbing alcohol works best for me. Just wipe on full strength and then wash off.

Beachy1

HOW TO REMOVE MOLD FROM WALLS

If the walls are painted, there are several solutions. Easiest and cheapest: Wash the walls with dilute bleach, then rinse thoroughly and allow to dry. The bleach kills the mold spores. To prevent it from returning, make sure the room has loads of ventilation when it's steamy and paint with a product designed to cope with steamy atmospheres; these contain a mold inhibitor. If it's not a bathroom, then there is a condensation problem that needs to be addressed to prevent mold from returning. Condensation always goes to the coldest part of the wall.

triplikate

HOW TO STACK KNIVES IN THE DISHWASHER

Always stack knives blade down in the dishwasher so they can't slash an unwary elbow as it reaches past.

Cali

HOW TO REMOVE MASCARA STAINS FROM CARPET

Use a small amount of turpentine on a soft cloth and rub gently; it does work.

Redlady

HOW TO ALWAYS HAVE A NEW GARBAGE BAG READY

Keep your roll of garbage bags in the trash can, under the present bag, so that when you take it out full, the new ones are handy underneath.

redfifi

HOW TO ARRANGE YOUR BEDROOM FOR THE BEST LIGHTING TO DO YOUR MAKEUP

Buy a dressing table with a mirror attached (even if it's from a thrift shop) and place it in front of a window. That way you have all your makeup on the table in front of you, and you have natural light for applying your makeup. I have one in my room and I don't know what I'd do without it.

bekki007

HOW TO GET BUBBLES OUT OF WALLPAPER THAT HAS DRIED ON THE WALL

Get a really thin pin and poke it in the bubble; then *slowly* push out the air using a towel or cloth. Ta-da, bubble gone.

If you take the air out too quickly or if you use your fingers, you will end up with a crease.

madz

HOW TO GET SCREW ANCHORS OUT OF WALLS

Screw a larger screw into the anchor, then grip it with pliers and pull in a circular motion.

Ally1310

HOW TO GET YOUR MAN TO PUT UP A SHELF

You: "Can you put the drill on to charge please, sweetie."

Him: "Why?"

You: "I need a shelf put up and I think it is high time I started to do these things for myself, darling."

Him: "Er . . . you haven't done this before?"

You: "No my love, but I hate having to ask you to carry out these tasks for me."

Him: "Don't worry about it. I will put the shelf up for you. These drills aren't all that easy to use."

You: "Why thank you, my angel!"

Just used this ploy and it worked like a dream!

ladydigger

HOW TO PAINT WALLS QUICKLY

Forget using rollers, which splash, and paint pads, which you have to keep dipping and wiping in the paint tray. Get a large car-cleaning type of sponge and cut it in half. Wear rubber gloves and dip the sponge in the paint before lightly "scrubbing" the wall with it. It is really, really fast (although you may have to give the wall another coat when the first is dry). You should get two decorating sponges out of one large sponge, and of course you simply throw them away afterward instead of having to clean them with loads of water. Just tried this and painted a huge wall in about three minutes! It was very even, too.

ladydigger

HOW TO PICK AN INEXPENSIVE CARPET

Seagrass matting is great cheap carpet. It's really low maintenance and looks nice for years.

SamanthaCameron

HOW TO HIDE PESKY CABLES

If you can, get them to run along the sides of the walls and cover them with cheap cord covering material (bias binding is perfect). They will look far better than black or white plastic. The covering will also protect the cable.

LucyD

HOW TO CLEAN BLACK MOLD FROM THE RUBBER SEAL ON A WASHING MACHINE

Try mixing hot water and lemon juice, then scrubbing with a soft toothbrush. I did this for the seal on my fridge.

7thsin

HOW TO CLEAR HOLES IN A NONSTICK IRON WHEN THE INSTRUCTIONS SAY NOT TO USE ANY PRODUCT IN THE WATER CHAMBER

I add some white vinegar to the water and leave to steam. It does clear the holes.

Redlady

HOW TO STOP WORRYING ABOUT LEAVING THE IRON ON

Get into the habit of unplugging electrical equipment when you finish using it. That way you'll be certain. Especially with something like an iron, where you can not only unplug it, but also put it away. Tidy and safe.

superfairy

As soon as you finish ironing, switch it off and pull out the plug. As you look at your hand pulling the plug out, say to yourself, "It's Monday (or whatever day it is) and I am unplugging the iron." It sounds a bit weird, but it sticks in your mind and reassures you if you start to worry about the iron later in the day.

bluebell11

HOW TO DEODORIZE YOUR WASHING MACHINE

Fill the detergent dispenser with vinegar and run a wash cycle on an empty machine. This both cleans and deodorizes the washing machine. It works in the dishwasher too *and* removes lime scale.

ashling

HOW TO FOLD FITTED SHEETS NEATLY BY YOURSELF

Fold in one pair of fitted ends and close them in a drawer—this is your "other person." Then step back and fold in the other corners, pull sharply, walk toward the drawer, and tuck that end in as well. Keep repeating until the sheet is a neat size, et voila! A perfectly folded sheet.

Ali161

HOW TO GET BUBBLEGUM OUT OF FABRIC

Put the item of clothing in the freezer. Once it is frozen, the bubblegum will peel off quite easily and shouldn't leave a mark.

mimi18

HOW TO KEEP A BED LINEN SET TOGETHER

Keep your matching bedding in one of the pillowcases. Easy to identify and when you need to change the bed, everything is together.

patsharp

HOW TO MAKE OLD TOWELS SOFT AGAIN

White vinegar seems to be *the* multipurpose household product. Add some to your laundry cycle and it will refluff your towels.

LucyD

HOW TO GET UNDERARM STAINS OUT OF CLOTHES

Baking soda works wonders for this. The night before you are going to wash those particular shirts, mix equal parts of baking soda and water. Dip the stained part of the shirt in the mixture and then stick it in a bag until you are ready to wash it. The stains will come out and the shirt will smell very fresh.

Jillaroo95

HOW TO CLEAN BALLPOINT PEN STAINS FROM LEATHER

I used hair spray on my leather sofa and it worked very well. Spray just a little at a time and rub gently with a damp cloth.

luckywhite

HOW TO PREPARE TO MOVE

Here is my big moving tip: When you put stuff in boxes, label what drawers they came from—e.g., Bottom Right Kitchen Drawer—not where you're going to put stuff in your new home. It makes finding things in a sea of identical brown boxes a lot easier, as you'll remember where they where in your old place and be able to find the relevant box.

bekki007

HOW TO TRANSPORT BOOKS WHEN MOVING

Instead of creating lots of incredibly heavy boxes full of books, stack them and tie them with string, like you would a parcel. Then you have little stacks that aren't too heavy and that can fit into small spaces and corners when you're packing the car.

Luda

HOW TO ASK GOOD QUESTIONS BEFORE RENTING
AN APARTMENT

1. Financial: Rent, deposit (including repayment conditions, interest-bearing account), lease document, term (month-to-month, annual), insurance, included utilities (water, gas, electric, TV).
2. Maintenance: Who fixes what? who takes out the garbage? On-site superintendent, off-site management company, or are you supposed to wake the landlord?
3. Move-in/DIY rules: Can you move furniture in only during certain hours? Certain days? using designated elevators? Can you paint the walls? Replace the ugly sink fixture?
4. Security: Who gets keys to your doors? Are there parking, neighborhood crime issues?
5. Quality of life: Are there rules regarding pets, washer/dryer, children, older people, noise; is the elevator reliable? Do local restaurants deliver food? Is transit nearby?

Last, without the landlord around, ask the neighbors candidly what they like most/least.

DezG

HOW TO KEEP A FIRE GOING

Keep your old wine corks. One or two thrown onto the dying embers will definitely perk it up again.

Motherknowsbest

HOW TO GUARD AGAINST FIRE

Never, ever leave either a glass paperweight or magnifying glass where sunlight can shine on it through a window. The concentrated beam could start a fire in a few minutes.

Gam

Life

or Any other business.

*L*ife, the universe, and everything . . . but it's the "everything" that's the problem really. Most of the challenges life throws at us are not existential, but about how to get your neighbors to shut up, how to respond to a rude question, and how to stop your glasses from steaming up on a cold day. The measurable quality of a day normally hangs on the ability to get the answers to those questions right, rather than discovering the answer to "Is there a God and, if so, what was He thinking?" Leading a good life is to a large extent composed of small but crucial decisions. None of which could be classified as important, but taken together, they have the most profound impact on your experience.

HOW TO PLAY A GREAT TRICK FOR APRIL FOOLS' DAY

Here's a brilliant idea for a subtle but effective revenge tactic that is also good for April Fools. Turn every battery from every appliance in the house the wrong way around, including the TV remote, mouse, radios, power tools . . .

Abi1973

The night before, put all the clocks in your house forward an hour; then lie back and listen as everyone else panics in the morning.

Esme

Add food coloring to the milk in your fridge.

JoanG

HOW TO BE GOOD

If it's not nice, not true, and not necessary, don't say it.

gemini

HOW TO COPE WITH SCARY MOVIES WITHOUT RUNNING OUT, CLOSING YOUR EYES, OR GENERALLY SQUIRMING

Start by opening your eyes! Uncover those ears. Look at every little detail of the movie—the props, outfits, lighting, and so on. Anything that scares you, challenge with, "Wow, that's great makeup/special effects." Once you notice every little detail, reality comes back into perspective.

pandsy

HOW TO DEAL WITH A GROUP OF YOUNG BOYS PLAYING FOOTBALL IN THE STREET RIGHT OUTSIDE YOUR HOUSE

Try dropping stink bombs (which you can buy from any good joke shop) in the area. Although you might have to put up with the smell for a bit, it will see them off.

S123

HOW TO GET NEIGHBORS TO BE QUIET

I have had neighbors who regularly held noisy parties in their garden late at night. I would open my windows and play either classical or cheesy music quite loudly—they soon got the message.

Englishchick

HOW TO DEVELOP BETTER HANDWRITING

My mom always said that the key to neat handwriting is keeping all of the letters the same size, so that the tops of the a, e, o, u, y, n, etc. are all in a straight line. Sounds simple but it's true.

AliFlump

HOW TO GET REVENGE ON A BITCHY PERSON WHEN
IGNORING HER DOESN'T WORK

A simple "My, aren't we being rude/grumpy/bitchy today!" has worked for me in the past. You might also try "I see you are flexing your inner bitch/witch today, well done!" or "I see your parents forgot to teach you any manners and social skills." Don't shout it, but say it loud enough so you can be heard—hopefully by a few people, including your bitchy person.

valentine

HOW TO GET RID OF A PUSHY SALESMAN

If he's one of those dreaded people on the doorstep wanting you to change your oil company (or something equally irritating), just wait for a pause in the spiel and politely say, "I'm not interested, thank you, and I'm shutting the door now." He'll no doubt try to talk over you, but you're quite justified in shutting the door in his face. If he's actually in your house, one of the best weapons you can use is silence. Don't provide him with an objection to overcome and he'll eventually flounder and you can usher him out.

LindaCee

HOW TO GIVE A SINCERE APOLOGY

Eye contact—no matter how hard it is, look the person in the eye. It's a matter of respect.

Megalle925

Think about exactly what you did wrong and why it was wrong. Say these points first. Explain that you know you were wrong and that you feel guilt and sadness about what you did. Follow up a verbal apology with a written one. Under no circumstances make a joke. After the apology allow the other person some time to think before you contact him or her again. Do not ask if you're forgiven.

charliamio

HOW TO RESPOND TO A RUDE QUESTION

I ask for the question to be repeated. Mentally you can smack the person with an invisible spade, but in reality it is best to say, "Could you repeat the question?" You can then reply with, "Why do you want to know?" This is polite, yet it will probably make the person blush as he or she will look rude and crass to the people around you.

bakewell

HOW TO PREVENT GLASSES FROM STEAMING UP WHEN GOING INSIDE IN COLD WEATHER

If you can see without them for a bit, put your glasses in your pocket before or after going inside so they adjust to the heat quicker.

xXxLeannexXx

HOW TO COPE WITH TURNING THIRTY-SIX

Think of the alternative! A friend of mine lost her sister to stomach cancer; the sister was thirty-four when she died. Does that help?

If you are feeling bad about hitting thirty-six (you young thing!), then take the opportunity to rethink your life, career, relationship/s, etc. If there's anything you don't like about your life, try to make small changes to improve it.

COLIYTYHE

HOW TO FEEL ATTRACTIVE WHEN YOU'RE IN YOUR FORTIES AND BEGINNING TO FEEL OLD, UNSEXY, AND BORING

Why not do something "naughty" like taking pole-dancing lessons? They are quite widely available nowadays and are fantastically good exercise. Enlist a couple of girlfriends and go have a ball while toning up your backside—it's guaranteed to make you feel more alive and sexy. The great thing about being in your forties is that you can *finally* do something fun like this without being crippled by teenage self-consciousness, or worrying for a second what the rest of the world thinks!

BooBoo

This is tough, but it helps to refocus your perspective: You will never be younger than you are today, your hair will only get grayer, your skin will only get more wrinkly. So, if you think about it—you're peaking! Make the most of it and don't waste a day.

Vivian

HOW TO CELEBRATE TURNING FORTY WITHOUT BREAKING THE BANK

Make the celebration occur over a year—make a list of things you've always wanted to do but have never gotten around to (for example, reading a particular classic you've never gotten through before, learning how to knit, running five miles nonstop, making a perfect soufflé, building a piece of furniture). Then work on one of these each month of your birthday year and make it a year of achievement.

Jillaroo95

HOW TO TEACH YOURSELF TO ACT RESPONSIBLY AND THINK BEFORE ACTING

Start by deliberately waiting at least one full breath every time you have to answer a question/make a move/make a choice. That one breath may seem like a long time to pause and consider what you're doing, but it saves lots of time later in regret. Basically, keep breathing to keep yourself calm and thoughtful.

tiptoetipster

HOW TO APPEAR CALM WHEN YOU'RE BURNING UP WITH RAGE

In an ideal world, relax your body. If you're too angry to do that, then try to stop clenching obvious parts of your body (e.g., fists or jaw) and transfer that tension to somewhere the other person can't see (e.g., curl up toes or clench buttocks). Biting the inside of your lip can force you to stop clenching your jaw, which is a real giveaway.

Make your eyes smile slightly (not too much or you look like a maniac; just enough that you appear relaxed and confident). Unless you're feeling calm enough, don't smile with your mouth, it will freeze and make you look more anxious/angry.

Concentrate on relaxing your belly so that the breath can go all the way into your lungs, which will help calm you down anyway.

feebz152

HOW TO STOP WORRYING ABOUT EVERYTHING AND JUST ENJOY LIFE

A good way to put things into perspective is to ask yourself, How much will this matter six months from now?

Magda

HOW TO DEAL WITH SHORT-FUSED PEOPLE

Walk away after saying that you aren't going to talk to them while they are shouting/swearing etc. Usually there is no reasoning with such people. You have to walk away and give them time to think better about what they are doing. People have to realize that acting like a child is not going to get them what they want and, indeed, will make things harder for them as people won't want to be around them.

DOZIGGY

HOW TO BE LESS ARGUMENTATIVE

This may sound lame but it really works. Whenever you feel angry or as though you're about to start an argument, do a slow count from ten backwards in your head, then take a deep breath and just talk calmly or walk away.

nickiebabesx

HOW TO STOP COMPLAINING AND START ENJOYING LIFE

I think to a great degree, we're all in a position to decide whether or not we're going to be happy people. Try not to dwell on the stuff that's wrong in your life. The phrase "count your blessings" is a bit hackneyed, but it's true—concentrate on all the things that are good in your life, like great family, good friends, nice house, good job, etc. You do yourself no favors by being negative and pessimistic, and it's a sure-fire way to drive people away from you.

LindaCee

HOW TO COPE WITH BEREAVEMENT

How close you were to the deceased will pretty much dictate how you cope. The closer you were, the harder it is. It is over three years since my young son died and I don't feel anywhere near coping with it, really. Allow yourself time and accept that there is no right or wrong way to act or react. Don't be afraid to tell friends if you're having a bad day/time; let them help. You will be told that everything you feel is normal—which might even make you angry—but it is true—there are so many emotions you have to go through, so many different stages. But one piece of advice—live! Make sure you make the most of your life in honor of your lost loved one; live for them.

COLIYTYHE

Be honest, but brief, when people ask you how you are. If you always put on a brave face, people won't be so eager to offer help. Equally, if you give them an hour's commentary on why you are so miserable, they won't come back.

Don't be afraid to ask for practical help, especially in the early days, and be specific. For instance, ask people to take you out and amuse you for the day, so you are forced to interact with the world again, and remind yourself that life goes on, even if you are not yet ready to move on with it.

villanova

HOW TO WRITE A CONDOLENCE/SYMPATHY NOTE

My father passed away in 1994, and the words from one note I received still stay with me to this day: "I know how difficult this is to accept."

The note was from someone who had just lost her own father, and I can't tell you how much it touched me. It is indeed so hard to believe that the person you've loved your whole life is really gone. I've used those seven words in many sympathy notes since then. I hope they help you, too.

susieq76

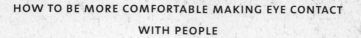

HOW TO BE MORE COMFORTABLE MAKING EYE CONTACT WITH PEOPLE

Look at the space between their eyes instead of trying to look into both eyes. I have the same problem and no one ever notices!

JessyIdol

HOW TO BE MORE ASSERTIVE AND TURN PEOPLE DOWN

This just takes practice, and the trick is to say no. Just "no" or "Sorry, I can't." No further explanation as to why you can't; that way you only go down a rat hole. You may have to repeat the "Sorry, I just can't" sentence a few times before people get the idea. It worked for me. If you're not happy saying this then say, "I will have to think about it and I'll get back to you shortly." It's the long-winded explanations of why you can't do something that make you feel trapped into saying yes.

ashling

HOW TO BOOST YOUR SELF-ESTEEM

Look outside yourself. Find ways to contribute to others through charities, church, your children's school, etc. By helping others or contributing to projects, you will forget about whether you are adequate or not and have concrete evidence (when you find time to look) of your value. You will also be setting a good example for your children, and they will be proud of their more well-rounded parent.

hjason

HOW TO DRAW ATTENTION TO YOURSELF AT A SOCIAL EVENT

Greet people even if you don't know them; they will notice you the rest of the evening.

Dine

HOW TO GET PEOPLE TO NOTICE YOU AND LIKE YOU MORE

Relax. Stop being so self-conscious. And read some interesting books so you have intriguing things to say. I always get an audience when I talk about how fascinating I find slime mold to be . . .

Josa2

HOW TO MAKE A GOOD FIRST IMPRESSION

When entering a room, twist or push the door handle down before pushing to open the door. This should make sure you come into the room with your face tilted up rather than focused on the door knob.

feebz152

HOW TO BEGIN A CONVERSATION WITH THE VERY OLD OR ILL

Try "Can I ask your advice about something?" Just invent a problem—how to roast a chicken, where is the best place to shop, does my butt look big in this—anything you like. Being asked for advice is a friendly compliment to someone. It makes them feel useful and knowledgeable. The elderly are frequently on the receiving end of the helping hand through no fault of their own, and it gives people a lift to know that they are valued and still able to help the world go round.

ladydigger

I so agree with you. My father is ninety-seven and his only grumble is that he feels so helpless and useless when he sees someone (usually me) doing something he feels unable to do, like the gardening. Asking his advice and telling him how useful it is obviously makes him feel good. Asking his advice on lots of levels (whether I want or need it or not) makes him feel valued and wise (which he is). Remember how much more old people know than we do. They've probably been through more than we ever will.

doingmybest

HOW TO FIND INTERESTING SUBJECTS TO TALK ABOUT

My no-fail conversation-starter is natural disasters. When I'm with people I don't know very well, I bring this up. It gets interesting, particularly when you have people from different areas.

I live in earthquake country and have had all sorts of interesting conversations with folks, comparing the experience of living with earthquakes versus living with other disasters. Once I was at a conference and sitting at a large round table with a bunch of people I didn't know. I started the conversation, and eventually our table was three people thick with others who wanted to join in.

Jillaroo95

HOW TO KEEP FROM CRYING IN PUBLIC

Pushing your tongue to the roof of your mouth hard works well, and try rubbing hard above your upper lip—this also works for some reason.

Hefzi

If you're arguing a point, just remember that you lose a massive amount of ground as soon as you start to cry. Keep control and you'll be taken a whole lot more seriously.

TizzysMum

HOW TO KNOW HOW MUCH TO GAMBLE

If you can't afford to give it away, then don't gamble it.

Catrine

Don't gamble, buy shoes!

fluffyfox

HOW TO COPE WITH LONELINESS

I remember only too well a time in my life when I felt so lonely, and it was awful. I took on a second job in a bar to make extra cash and get out of the gross apartment I lived in alone, and also applied to be a helper on the adult literacy program run by the local council. I felt I was helping other people, which gave me a sense of satisfaction, I was earning a few extra dollars in the bar, and I had somewhere else to go rather than staying in that depressing apartment alone.

numptieheid

HOW TO BE BETTER AT WAKING UP AND GETTING OUT OF BED IN THE MORNING

Just open your eyes and get up ASAP, without thinking about it. I find that if I walk around and leave my room, the need to get back into bed will fade. If you can get to the kitchen without hurting yourself in your half-awake state, even better.

2sqrrd

HOW TO HAVE ENOUGH TIME TO COMPLETE DAY-TO-DAY TASKS WHEN IT SEEMS YOU NEVER GET ANYTHING DONE

Set yourself one task at a time and give yourself time to do it, say twenty minutes. Set a timer clock and get going. You will be surprised how much you get through.

Redlady

HOW TO DEAL WITH A PRANK PHONE CALL

Buy a whistle and blow it as hard as you can down the phone. They will get the message.

bekki007

Look up the procedure for reporting such calls to your local police department and phone company. (Often this can be found in your local phone book.) During the next call, say something like "I have contacted my local police and telephone carrier to report these harassing phone calls. Stop now or I shall take all available legal action against you." Then hang up; do not engage in dialogue. If you feel it is appropriate (the calls are scary, mean-spirited, make you feel stalked), *do* contact the police and phone company. They can trace numbers (even ones your caller ID cannot) and take action. Calls can best be traced at the time they are made, with a tracer in place, so don't delay lodging a complaint if the calls are getting frightening.

DezG

Just lay the receiver down and leave it. As the person receiving the call, it's up to you to cut it off, so keep the caller waiting as long as possible. You could even say, "Please hang on, I'll be back in a minute."

Ally1310

HOW TO LOOK GOOD IN PHOTOS

Point your chin slightly down and angle your face to the side a little. Look at the person taking the picture (a few inches above the camera) and your eyes will look a little bigger without red-eye.

bakewell

Look into the camera and say "Hi there!" really enthusiastically, as though you've just seen a great friend. It really works.

Tooke

HOW TO PREVENT LOSING YOUR CAMERA

Take a photo of your contact details at the beginning of every memory card. If you lose your camera the finder will know how to find you to give it back.

Ruth

HOW TO BE CONFIDENT SINGING IN FRONT OF PEOPLE

My mother, who was an opera singer, always told me to put my hand on the corner of the piano, or to hold something small that fit in the palm of my hand. I don't know why this worked, but it did. It took my mind off the people in front of me. Instead I concentrated on rolling this thing in my hand.

Pienkfly

HOW TO LEARN TO FLOAT

First you have to be comfortable in the water—having water in your ears, letting it splash on your face, etc. Stand in shallow water so you don't panic. Next, have a friend support you as you recline in the water (his/her hands under your lower back/butt and shoulders). Lie down in the water with your feet outstretched and your arms in a T shape or above your head, stick your belly out, and don't let your butt drop. Lie there supported by your friend until you are comfortable. Then tell your friend to slowly let go (moving his/her hands away so you feel less support, more float). You're floating! (May take several tries.)

DezG

A simple tip: Butt up and ears in the water—it keeps your body level.

LindaCee

HOW TO OVERCOME APPREHENSION

If you're terrified or even phobic about a future engagement such as a dentist appointment, try this: Repeat in your mind or even out loud what you are afraid of, such as "I've got to go to the dentist," for about fifteen minutes. Before you know it, your mind has wandered onto something else. It takes the terror out of the thought.

Bradley

When you start to feel anxious do some deep breathing. The out breath should be longer than the in breath. Ideally a count of seven on the in breath and eleven on the out breath.

AKB

HOW TO OVERCOME SHYNESS

The thing to remember about shyness is that it tends to go away once you take that first step. Try easing yourself into whatever you're shy of. For example, if you're shy about approaching people, make it your business to say something to five strangers a day, even if it's just "Good morning!" or "Wow, isn't the view brilliant?" Close your eyes, take a deep breath, and say to yourself, "Nothing bad will happen to me"; then go do it. What's the worst that could happen?

estuans_interius

Money

or As my grandmother said, "Money is very good for the nerves."

Wedding speeches are often tearjerkers. Declarations of undying love get me every time. But the all-time most romantic line I have ever heard was when the husband of a dear friend and colleague said, "You never need to open another bill." It's not that he is fantastically rich; he was just offering to relieve her of the hassle of dealing with the things. We all hate pressing and unpleasant financial matters, so it is an act of supreme love to remove the need to open the ominous envelopes. There are huge numbers of people who believe, as an act of faith, that if they put bills in their handbag or desk drawer, they won't be there tomorrow. Denial is undeniably fun. Until the repo man comes.

HOW TO SETTLE WITH COLLECTION AGENCIES SO YOUR CREDIT RATING ISN'T AFFECTED

Don't bury your head in the sand; get in contact with the agency. They have dealt with many situations and will have an option that you can live with.

Think about ways you can save money in everyday life that will help you pay your debts faster. There is great advice/support on the moneysavingexpert.com site and forums.

Do *not* go to those consolidation companies or take advice from a loan provider; their interest is getting you to take more credit, and there are other ways you should consider first.

Be proud of yourself for taking the first step to a debt-free existence, and be patient while it gets sorted out.

Catrine

HOW TO GET OUT OF DEBT

Remember to concentrate the bulk of your monthly payments on the credit cards you are paying interest on. If you've any interest-free cards, just pay the minimum and concentrate on clearing the cards that are actively adding to your debt.

LindaCee

HOW TO GET A LOAN WHEN BANKS ARE RARELY LENDING

Proof of being a low-risk credit customer with a good payment record on any car loans or credit card payments and a secure salaried job will help—as will a financially sound guarantor who will guarantee your loan repayment.

connyosb

HOW TO AVOID IMPULSE BUYING

I make a preshopping trip every season. I walk around the stores just to look at the new styles and decide what I will need. I don't carry more then $20 in cash and I leave my credit card at home so I won't be tempted to overspend. I have no problem telling the salesperson that I'm just looking. This is when I try things on to see what brands fit well. Then I go back the next week with my credit card. It's amazing how many things are not as appealing when you wait a week.

Masi

HOW TO BEAT SHOPPING ADDICTION

Put your credit cards in a tin can filled with water and put it in the freezer. That way you can't put it in the microwave to thaw it out. When you see that "must have" outfit, bag, or pair of shoes, salivate over them but don't buy yet. Tell yourself you will buy them in one week's time. During that week think about the "must have" item, imagine it in your wardrobe, and consider how it will make your life complete. If after a week you still desire it as much as you did on day one, then buy it, but pay for it in cash. If, however, you no longer feel as strongly about it, put that same amount of money in a savings account and see how good you feel about yourself.

Annwae

Avoid stores. Sounds so simple, but it's so effective. If you have a lunch hour, read a book or go for a run, or something similar. I used to go to stores at lunch and it just put temptation in my way.

scottishchic

HOW TO STOP YOURSELF FROM FRITTERING AWAY ALL YOUR MONEY ON NOTHING

For one month starting on payday, keep a diary of everything you buy—from the weekly household shopping to a chocolate bar! At the end of the month, look back, and you will feel guilty/shocked about how much money you've pretty much thrown away. For the next month, when you want to spend money on useless stuff, move that money from your checking account to a savings account—your savings will build up in no time, and the cash isn't in a checking account tempting you to spend. It's hard to get used to but it's made a huge difference to my lifestyle.

scottishchic

HOW TO SAVE MONEY ON DRY CLEANING

Read the label in your clothes! If it says "Dry Clean," it is just a suggestion and it means that you can wash the garment yourself—but do so carefully. If it says "Dry Clean Only," it is pretty much an order, and you risk damaging the garment if you launder it any other way.

Tooke

HOW TO SPEND LESS ON DISPOSABLE SWIM DIAPERS FOR BABIES AND TODDLERS

Don't throw away your "disposable" swim diapers. They will rinse through and dry so can be worn a few times. They can even be put through the washing machine on a gentle wash. They're great for vacations because you don't need to take as many as you would if you were to chuck them out after each swim.

Spendspendspend

HOW TO SAVE MONEY FOR YOUR DAUGHTER WHEN YOU ARE USELESS AT SAVING AND SPEND LIKE THERE'S NO TOMORROW

Open a bank account for her—in her own name—so only she can access the money, and set up a direct debit from your account to hers.

squirrel

HOW TO SAVE MONEY

Getting together with a few friends in similar financial circumstances and agreeing to save X amount of money every week is another way of saving. Like a diet club, if you can encourage and remind each other, you can do it.

LucyD

If you're creating a budget for yourself, don't be too strict. It's a little bit like a rigid diet—if it's too extreme, it only makes you more inclined to fall off the wagon! The more realistic you can be with your goals, the better it will work.

LucyD

I discovered this top tip yesterday by accident!

I had gone to the supermarket to do my weekly shopping, carrying only my debit card. Thinking I could grab a huge shopping cart and have a good browse, I found that all the carts were being used; I was forced to use one basket only. Not only did I get round the market quickly as my arms ached, I also ended up spending a lot less than I would have had I been browsing. I also came home with exactly what was on the list!

> *raefaye*

Eat before you shop. It's very simple and it works.

> *madz*

If you always do your grocery shopping on the same day every week, try shopping one day later each week (with the same list), and over seven weeks you'll have saved one week's worth of your shopping.

> *amontanini*

My first stop in the supermarket is the section with the reduced items. Try to figure out what time they make their reductions—it may be 6:30 or 8 p.m., but it can be worth checking out and changing the way you shop.

> *Ally1310*

Parenting — the Early Years

or Damage limitation.

On becoming pregnant for the first time, the most important thing to do is to ignore your friends—everyone will cluster and, particularly those who have had children, will display tribal glee that someone else is about to suffer. Being a parent is hard, but not that hard; it's also amazing and uplifting and worth it. With the right kind of advice (which is practical), it can be even easier. Above all, carefully laid plans just don't work. What works is the acceptance that from now on your life will be a bit more disorderly than you might want. And, possibly for the first time in your life, you will have to accept that you can't do everything. Recognize that you can't be Super Mom, and move on. You have to agree not to be perfect, although these tips will help you get close.

HOW TO BE RELAXED WITH YOUR FIRST BABY

Try to leave the baby alone with someone else within the first few days, so this doesn't become something you and your partner start to fear. As much as the baby has to get used to being with someone else, you have to get used to it, too.

Esme

HOW TO SURVIVE WITH A BRAND-NEW BABY

In the first days after the birth, lots of people will want to visit. It's your partner's job to keep unwanted visitors away and to do so with diplomacy. Remember, everyone wants to be kind, so treat them with kindness but be firm. You are likely to be exhausted and want lots of quiet time for bonding with your baby and getting used to the new routine. At the same time, do not shun close relatives who want to feel involved, and don't be shy about asking friends to help you with household chores, such as loading the dishwasher, or just making a cup of tea. You will literally have your hands full.

JoanG

HOW TO CALM A CRYING BABY

A crying baby is often calmed by being held across your tummy and having his or her bottom patted to the rhythm of a beating heart. At the last stages before birth their bottoms sit just under your heart, so mimicking this is very reassuring to them.

Emerald

Try swaddling the baby in a blanket; they often don't like their arms and legs being able to wave around too much. Being wrapped up makes them feel more secure.

bekki007

You need to go through the checklist first: changing, feeding, too hot or too cold. Putting them in a warm bath sometimes does the trick, and babies love to be massaged just as we do. Put the baby on your lap on a big towel, dim the lights, and gently massage away with some baby oil. If all this fails, a drive in the car seems to work. It passes . . .

patsharp

HOW TO CURE YOUR BABY'S THRUSH INEXPENSIVELY

If your baby has thrush (white tongue) frequently, get a bottle of gentian violet from the pharmacy (less than a dollar) and use a cotton swab to paint it on the baby's tongue and insides of his cheeks. (Gentian violet stains badly, so don't dress him in anything nice for a few days, because his drool will be purple!) This got rid of thrush for good for both my babies after the expensive stuff the doctor prescribed only got rid of it temporarily.

asildem

HOW TO REMOVE CRADLE CAP

Gently massage your baby's head using a soft bristle baby hair brush while washing his hair with his regular shampoo. It doesn't hurt and is very effective at removing cradle cap.

> *welshlass*

Use breast milk. It's naturally healing.

> *M*

HOW TO KEEP YOUR BABY CHANGING AREA CLEAN

If you suspect your baby has a seriously dirty diaper, place a clean one underneath his bottom before taking the old one off.

> *Esme*

HOW TO CALM A SCREAMING TODDLER

This is one I often used with success with my little Montessori pupils. Get down to their eye level and speak to them in a very low, calm voice. They have to stop screaming to hear what you say, and they usually do.

> *ashling*

Apparently we all need to be understood—If you mirror a toddler's words and feelings in a calm voice (even if it feels silly), it shows that you "get it" and it calms them down.

twink

HOW TO CALM BABIES OR TODDLERS

While I was pregnant I put a favorite soothing tune on my mobile phone and when sitting down resting, I played the music to my bump. After I had my son, whenever he got stressed out or upset I played that music to him, and hey presto, he calmed right down.

nzrocks

HOW TO KEEP YOUR TODDLERS SOCKS ON

All toddlers like to remove their socks in a concerted campaign to lose them and cause hypothermia. Put thick tights on them instead with trousers over the top, and their sock removal activities will be at an end. This works very well on my two-and-a-half-year-old son.

Malcolm

HOW TO CONVINCE A TODDLER TO BRUSH HIS
TEETH PROPERLY

I used to look after two wonderful little boys who weren't that keen on brushing their teeth, so I made getting the sparkliest teeth into a competition. They would rush to the bathroom, brush, and come dashing back to show me, and I would pretend to be blinded by their teeth shining like pearls, covering my eyes and falling back on the couch. They would shriek with laughter and the winner would get to pick their bedtime story. Every night was a draw so they got a story each.

valentine

HOW TO GET YOUR CHILDREN TO USE DENTAL FLOSS

My son's gums were bleeding after he'd just brushed his teeth so I asked him if he'd been diligent about flossing. When he said no, I asked, "Wouldn't it worry you if there were blood coming out of your eyes, ears, or nose?" He was horrified by this vivid picture and has been flossing ever since.

CeeVee

HOW TO GET YOUR BABY TO SLEEP THROUGH THE NIGHT

My baby kept waking because he would roll over and get stuck on his tummy when he slept in a baby sleeping bag. His dad tucked him in very tight with a blanket, and now he sleeps right through.

euston74

HOW TO GET A BABY/CHILD TO SLEEP

I bought a "white noise" CD, which worked. It works for exhausted parents, too!

sk1970

HOW TO STOP YOUR CHILD FROM GETTING OUT OF BED REPEATEDLY EVERY EVENING

Just put her straight back to bed. Don't talk to her or acknowledge her; just put her back in bed. She'll soon get the message.

bekki007

HOW TO GET YOUR CHILD TO SLEEP PAST 6 A.M. NO MATTER WHAT TIME HE GOES TO BED

Get a cute alarm clock and set it together every night, so your child knows what time is getting-up time. If s/he wakes up before it goes off, s/he knows it's not getting-up time yet, and can look at a book or play with a toy until it goes off. This worked great with my niece and nephew.

Beano

Very difficult—you can try making sure that no light gets past his curtains. After that, manipulating the alarm clock is the best way.

First morning, set the alarm for ten minutes before he usually wakes up and make sure you are standing right outside his door. When it goes off, go straight in and make a big fuss of him for staying in bed until the alarm sounded. After that, move the alarm clock ahead by five minutes or so each day, and within about ten days you should be able to get him to stay in his room until a reasonable hour.

Rosebudsmummy

HOW TO GET YOUR CHILD TO LISTEN TO A BEDTIME STORY

Children want to be engaged with their parents; it gives them security. So engage them in conversation about the book, asking open-ended questions. If a character in the book says or does something, ask the child what he thinks the character was thinking or feeling. There are no right or wrong answers; this isn't the time for an argument. Just lots of mutual reading and cozy talk. You can learn a lot about what your child is thinking and feeling by listening to his answers, plus you are building his conversational skills and preventing the development of test anxiety by getting him used to answering nonthreatening questions. End every day with cozy snuggle/reading time with Mom/Dad, tender talks, and lots of love.

asildem

HOW TO HELP CHILDREN SLEEP IN UNFAMILIAR HOTEL ROOMS

I purchase a bunch of very inexpensive glow sticks (from camping stores), which my children shake to light up. They have fun playing with them before bed and then have the security of a safe glowing light if they wake during the night. If your child is under three or inclined to chew things, you might hang them on something out of reach during sleep time. The gentle light will last all night.

sara10

HOW TO TOILET TRAIN A TWO-YEAR-OLD WHO WON'T USE A POTTY

All two-year-olds will work for something: M&Ms, small toys, raisins, etc. Do a deal, offer rewards. Start small, with a reward for agreeing to sit on the potty; then introduce rewards for performing. The ultimate reward is being free of diapers and having real underwear! Big celebration!

HELENCLARKJAMES

Two years old is still quite young, so it could be that he/she isn't ready yet. Things that worked for me included taking her to the bathroom with me every time that I went and describing what I was doing, plus never getting cross when accidents happened (essential but a tall order!). However, the best tip is to buy underwear with an absolute favorite character such as Winnie the Pooh. They will be thrilled and will not want to get Winnie dirty or wet!

vaunieathome

Two-year-olds can be very strong-willed, and if potty training is a control issue, you must pretend that it doesn't matter to you! Give the child the illusion of control, and make him feel he is choosing to use the potty. Manage him psychologically as though he were a difficult adult, but mix in lots of hugs, praise, and unconditional love. And always remember: This too will pass. No child ever went to college carrying a diaper bag.

asildem

HOW TO GET A CHILD TO EAT

If you have a friend with a child who is a good eater, invite them over for meals. Often when children see others eating without a fuss, they start to do the same.

lencke

I've always had set mealtimes at the dinner table. I serve *one* meal and the kids either eat it or starve until the next meal. I don't serve anything I know a particular child really hates, but I also don't indulge any food weirdness. If the child is hungry he will eat; if not, that's fine. No shouting, no big scene. Kids clear the table and that's it until the next meal is served. Absolutely no eating between meals. Never once did any of my children's pals come to my house and not follow suit with the rest of us. I did, however, have amazed mothers saying things like, "How on earth did you get him to eat that?"

numptieheid

Turn it into an apparently carefree game that kids won't see through, such as who can crunch carrots/cucumber/celery the loudest?

JoanG

Have a painting session, then offer a prize to any children who can find and eat foods (from a selection you have on hand) of each of the colors used in their artwork: red strawberries, blueberries, green grapes, yellow bananas, etc.

Emerald

Have them "eat a rainbow," as recommended by chefs: Have a picture of a rainbow on the fridge and offer your child a sticker for every shade of food he or she eats.

esme

Children are less likely to notice whole grains in toasted rather than untoasted bread.

abi1973

HOW TO GET CHILDREN TO EAT VEGETABLES

Make the vegetables into a funny-face pattern on the plate. For example: sprouts for eyes, a carrot nose, and peas lined up for a smiley mouth. I found this did the trick and works really well with fruit, too.

loulougirl

My friend pureed vegetables and mixed the puree with pasta sauce. Her son ate the meal and grew a tremendous liking for vegetables.

Pattiedog

HOW TO GET CHILDREN TO EAT FRUIT

Try having a color day. Tell your children you will eat only red vegetables and fruit on a certain day and see what they come up with.

Rachaelicious

WHAT TO DO FOR YOUR CHILDREN'S BIRTHDAY PARTIES

We had a great "junk party"—friends saved cereal boxes, big boxes, toilet paper rolls, everything. We rented out the church hall, set up tables with glue, paint, and glitter, and let the kids make whatever models they wanted. They had a fantastic time and took their models home with them. Just remember to tell them to come in old clothes!

pene

HOW TO GET SAND OUT OF A CHILD'S EYE

Get the child to look up and tilt his head to the side that has the sand in it, then slowly pour water from a pitcher into the eye beside the nose. The water will run across the eye, down the face, and onto the floor (so over a sink or tub is recommended). This should clear all the sand after a few pitchers.

bekki007

HOW TO CHEAPLY ENTERTAIN TWO KIDS, AGED FIVE AND SEVEN

Go on a nature walk and make them look out for different bugs and trees on the way. They could also take wax crayons and make tree rubbings.

fruityloop

Do you bake, even a little bit? Make a cake with them. Sure, you'll have a disaster to clean up in your kitchen, but kids love to cook and are seldom allowed to do most of the steps by themselves. Cakes don't require knives, so they could do it all.

Then they could take the cake to someone who is ill or even just a neighbor.

stelladore

HOW TO HAVE STYLISH KIDS

Let them wear what they want (assuming it's appropriate for the occasion). Making them style conscious at a young age will only make them more materialistic and shallow when they grow up. The happiest memories of my childhood did not include worrying about fashion or what I looked like. Now grown up, I worry about them a considerable amount (without pressure from my mother).

S123

HOW TO HELP CHILDREN GET THROUGH THE FEAR OF GETTING A SHOT

I've found it helpful to tell my kids to (a) turn their heads away from the arm getting the shot while (b) blowing out hard, as though blowing out a candle. The distraction of blowing out helps tremendously (I even do it myself!).

CeeVee

HOW TO KEEP YOUR HOME TIDY WITH KIDS

Having plenty of storage is the first thing. Make a game of tidying up. This works even for the smallest child. Set a timer for, say, three minutes and have a race to see who can tidy up the fastest. Have a put-things-back-before-you-take-a-new-thing-out rule. Have a periodic cleanup of broken toys and games they have grown out of.

ashling

HOW TO MAKE GREAT PLAY DOUGH

I love this recipe:

1 cup flour
1 cup warm water
2 tsp. cream of tartar
1 tsp. oil
1/4 cup salt

Mix all ingredients and stir over medium heat until the ball is not goopy. Color with food coloring after the dough has cooled.

agnes123

HOW TO NOT LOSE A CHILD WHILE OUT

My mother used to dress my brother and me in very bright matching clothes when traveling. This meant that even if we lost her, we could generally spot each other in the crowd. Not great for your street cred to have a younger sibling in the same get-up as you, but hey!

LucyD

HOW TO STOP LITTLE BOYS FROM FIGHTING

Have a long chat about why people go to war. They won't understand a word, but will be so bored they will stop fighting.

Tooke

HOW TO NOT SWEAR IN FRONT OF CHILDREN

It's easy to sound like a prig with most words that serve as bleeps, but if you regularly make fun of lustily and heartily letting fly in front of your children with a bellowing "Blow," "Blast," or "Oh, duck!" it will be habit-forming. And "poo" is nicely mock-shocking for kids.

Abi1973

HOW TO STOP SCREAMING AT THE KIDS

I think screaming at kids becomes a habit, one that I have
found very difficult to break. Because you shout, they shout
back, and before long there is a screaming match going on. Try
to catch yourself as you hear your voice getting louder; take a
second and bring it down a key. Very difficult initially but with
practice this gets easier. Now I find myself saying to my son,
"I'm not shouting at you, please don't shout at me." The pleasure I get from this is enormous.

   ets

Shouting at your children is as useful as stopping your car by
honking the horn—everyone looks, but it has no effect. My
child's teacher had more effect by lowering her voice than
raising it.

   happycanadian

HOW TO DISCUSS SEX WITH YOUR ELEVEN-YEAR-OLD
DAUGHTER

Relax and chat about it as if it were anything else. Choose a
time when you are both relaxed and comfortable. Answer all
her questions. Try the whole bananas and condoms thing—
she'll be really embarrassed but she'll thank you for it one day.
Well, she may not thank you, but she'll accept it eventually.

   FabulousFeminist

Parenting—it Never Ends

or Which of you is more freaked out that they're turning into you?

The far greater shock than giving birth and cutting the umbilical cord is the discovery, twenty-five years later, that it was never really cut at all. This will provoke mixed feelings in you, no matter how much you dreaded the empty nest. (And for previously unimaginable ambivalence, try having kids who are reluctant to leave the nest at all.) By this stage, if you're lucky, your children will be people you look forward to seeing more than anyone else in the world. At the same time, when they total the car, ask for yet another check, or fill your house with strangers gathered via Facebook, you will find yourself growling, "Enough already." Too bad, there's more to come. There's always more to come.

HOW TO GET YOUR TEENAGE DAUGHTER TO STOP HATING YOU

Wait however many minutes until she's over her fit? Or, seriously, just be a good parent and then wait until she's an adult and realizes what a good mother you were. Most of us don't like our mothers until we are of an age to appreciate what they've done for us (and that we've essentially become them).

stelladore

My mom used to tell me when I was a teenager, "It's not your parents you hate, but the power and control they have over you."

Yansipan

Hate is simply passion. She is saying she wants her own way with all the determination of a single-minded, hormone-fueled adolescent. I used to say to my daughter, "I simply don't accept that being a teenager means you are a special case. You need to behave in a decent manner." She seems to have turned out all right.

Josa2

HOW TO GET YOUR TEENAGERS TO COMMUNICATE

Take them out for lunch, coffee, or a walk and just talk casually before you ask what's up. If you keep things light they will open up. When they do, don't make a big deal out of anything they say, even if it does shock you there and then; just shrug and go on to something else. Then go back to it a while later and they will open up more.

sammyc

HOW TO COMMUNICATE WITH YOUR TEENAGERS

Try not to humiliate or shame them by listing their faults; it will make them feel judged, which is one of the things they hate most. Remember: You can't judge and listen at the same time.

twink

Don't make light of their problems. Try to see things from their point of view so that it makes sense to you, rather than dismissing them with "You're too young" or "You'll get over it."

suuse

HOW TO GIVE YOUR TEENAGE DAUGHTER MORE FREEDOM

Keep in mind that she won't learn any coping or problem-solving skills if you keep her wrapped in cotton. This is a really good time for her to learn them—while she's old enough to grasp what she's learning but still young enough to listen to you occasionally.

Jillaroo95

HOW TO GIVE YOUR TEENAGE DAUGHTER MORE FREEDOM
AND ACCEPT HER BOYFRIEND

Give her independence slowly so that you both can cope with the changes in your relationship. Accepting boyfriends is a tricky one, but you just have to do it; otherwise she will resent you. The first boyfriend probably won't last, and before you know it they will have broken up and you'll have all the tears to mop up. She'll keep you occupied and busy for a long time to come!

el

HOW TO GET YOUR DAUGHTER AWAY FROM A "BAD BOY"

If he isn't doing drugs or physically or mentally abusing her, then let the relationship run its course with minimum comment from you. Open your home to them (I don't necessarily mean for overnights, but just so she isn't skulking around outside the house.) Kill him with kindness and that will take the heat out of the rebellion, if that is what the relationship is about. Keep an eye on what's happening, but don't comment unless you're asked. She knows how you feel but keeping the door open for her is important.

ashling

HOW TO DECIDE WHAT IS THE RIGHT AGE TO ALLOW
YOUR DAUGHTER TO START SHAVING HER LEGS

The decision to start shaving legs should be made by the girl in question. It really has nothing to do with her parents at all (unless she is a toddler!). As for hair growing back thicker and darker after shaving, this is complete nonsense. If a teen feels self-conscious about hair on her legs, surely it is more favorable to shave regularly than have her obsess about something over which she has total control.

ladydigger

HOW TO HELP A GROWN CHILD WITH A BREAK-UP

Let him know that he's strong enough to get through this. Don't be too pushy or invasive. Be there for him without being overbearing, as this will, in most cases, simply cause irritation on your child's part. Also, never say anything along the lines of "I told you this wouldn't work. . . ." It might seem pretty obvious that one should avoid this, but some parents forget. Having your mistakes and faults pointed out to you after your heart has been stomped on does not make things any better.

dkarb

HOW TO MAKE YOUR GROWN SON WHO STILL LIVES AT HOME HELP AROUND THE HOUSE MORE AND SPEND A LITTLE TIME AS PART OF THE FAMILY

Make a date to have a proper chat with your son and tell him how you feel. Find out his point of view and see if you can reach a compromise on the housework front. It will be hard, but you must try very hard not to get upset or angry.

Try and set a family meal day, like Sunday lunch, at which you want to have the whole family eating around the table together. Open a bottle of wine and play at being the Waltons for a couple of hours. This is a great time to catch up on news, gossip, and so on.

Failing that, raise his rent, hire a cleaner, and go for a romantic dinner with your partner.

AmandaF

HOW TO COPE WITH AN EMPTY NEST

Keep in mind that your job as a mother was to raise your children so that they would become self-supporting. They have left the nest, so you have succeeded and should give yourself some considerable pats on the back. Take a class, join a group, or volunteer for a cause.

Jillaroo95

Pets

or The sane ones in the house (usually).

You can have some of the richest and most passionate relationships of your life with pets. Loving a lizard is perverse proof of the human capacity to love—we can project onto anything. Most of us give our pets voices (in the world I have created in my head, all horses talk just like James Mason) because it's the one and only thing they lack. They are reliable, predictable, sane, loving, and charming. There's just this one small catch—none of them, as yet, have been able to talk. So it's only a small favor to fill in the tiny little gap and bestow an Upper East Side accent upon your goldfish.

HOW TO GET A BIRD BACK INTO ITS CAGE

Draw the curtains and turn out the lights. Birds don't like to fly in the dark. You can then pick it up gently and put it back in the cage.

patsharp

HOW TO CATCH A MOTHER HEN AND HER CHICKS FREE-RANGING IN YOUR GARDEN

You are better off trying to catch them either late in the afternoon or early in the morning. They are a lot more settled at this time. Stand back so as not to spook them and then throw a towel over them. When you pick them up they will flap; be firm but gentle and hold their legs together.

felicitycp

HOW TO GET RID OF CAT SMELLS IN THE HOUSE

If you've got a cat that has peed or sprayed somewhere, clean the area with warm water mixed with some washing powder/ liquid. When the area has dried, sprinkle with a little vinegar to discourage the cat from using the area again. Always have one litter box per cat plus a spare. Cats are very fussy about sharing their toilet arrangements.

missgalore

HOW TO GET A YOUNG CAT TO STOP USING A LITTER BOX AND START GOING OUTDOORS

Sprinkle cat litter outside. He'll soon get the idea.

Lushlady

HOW TO STOP THE LOCAL FERAL CAT FROM USING THE CAT FLAP AND EATING ALL THE FOOD IN FRONT OF YOUR VERY TIMID CAT

A couple of years ago I had the problem of a feral tom breaking in and fighting my own cats. What I did was trap the feral and take him to the local cat rescue. I then paid for him to be neutered. This was much cheaper than all the trips I was making to the vet with my own cats! There was a happy ending in that he was eventually placed in a home.

MenopausalMadam

HOW TO STOP YOUR CAT FROM SCRATCHING THE WALLPAPER

Get an empty spray bottle (like the ones that bathroom cleaner or window cleaner comes in) and fill with water. Whenever the cat scratches, immediately squirt him/her with water. It won't harm the cat but will shock it enough to make it stop.

If you do that every time, he/she should eventually leave the wallpaper alone.

tanya123

If there is one area of the wall your cat always scratches, hang aluminum foil there for a few days. Cats hate the sound and feel of foil and they will not touch it or go anywhere near it. After a few days the cat will not go near the wall or area that he normally scratches, and you can remove the foil.

LibbyHews

HOW TO SUCCESSFULLY INTRODUCE A NEW KITTEN INTO THE HOME IF YOU ALREADY HAVE A DOG

Put the cat in a cat carrier (the ones with the wire door) and then take the dog (on a lead with someone it trusts holding it) into the room where the cat is. Do it in small stages, letting the dog sniff around the basket, and eventually let the cat out (with the dog still on the lead) to see how the dog reacts.

FlourescentAdolescent

HOW TO GET PET HAIR OFF YOUR FURNITURE

Use a rubber glove to remove pet hair from any fabric. Rub in one direction and the hair will lift and clump together.

ktigerlilly

HOW TO PREPARE A PET'S TRAVEL CRATE

When traveling, put an item of clothing that you have worn recently in your pet's carrier. Your smell will soothe him.

Clio

HOW TO STOP A DOG FROM PULLING ON THE LEAD WHEN FOOD, MUZZLES, AND HARNESSES DON'T STOP HIM

Take him somewhere safe and when he starts to pull, drop the lead and turn and walk the other way. Alternatively, you can use a long training leash if you don't want to drop the lead. Call him back to you and give him a treat when he comes. Keep repeating. He'll get the message that pulling on the lead is going to get him nowhere.

Ali161

HOW TO CURE A DOG'S BAD BREATH

You can buy charcoal biscuits in pet shops, little bone-shaped ones—my dogs love them and they help with bad breath.

valentine

HOW TO EASILY BRUSH A DOG WHO HATES IT

In one hand I hold his favorite treat so he can have just tiny nibbles. He's so preoccupied with getting the treat he barely notices I'm brushing him. Normally he would bite the brush or I would have an endless chasing frenzy.

pandsy

HOW TO GET YOUR DOG TO ACCEPT A NEW DOG

The best way to introduce a new dog is in a neutral area, not at home. Have a dog gate so they can sniff each other, but without the risk of a fight. You need to get your old dog to associate the new dog with good things, so give him treats and lots of fuss when the newcomer is around. The most important thing is to give them time and be patient; it may take weeks or months.

felicitycp

HOW TO GIVE YOUR DOG A SHINY COAT

Give him a little oil in his food every day. It can be vegetable or olive, whatever you have handy.

Jennynib

HOW TO HOUSE-TRAIN YOUR DOG WITHOUT
SPENDING MONEY

This takes loads of time, not loads of money. The advice given to me when I got a puppy was to take her out at regular intervals—every two to three hours, and always immediately after she eats, drinks a lot, or wakes up. You don't need money, just consistency.

stelladore

HOW TO STOP A DOGFIGHT

Tread hard on one of the feet of the dog whose jaws are locked on the other. Their yelp of pain will free the locked jaws.

ctussaud

My vet told me to get a stick and push it against the attacking dog's bottom!

patsharp

Cold water from a distance is definitely the best idea—it makes them jump enough that they'll separate even without your having to get too close. Turning a hose on them (if there's one handy) usually works best.

seagull-pie

HOW TO STOP DOGS FROM CHEWING ON THINGS

Purchase a bottle of clove oil (used for toothaches). With a paper towel, rub some oil on the article the dog has taken to chewing. Be careful because it is hot to the touch, but you can just wash it off with soap and water. The dog can't take the intense smell and stops chewing. It needs to be put on every couple of days, but suddenly the dog no longer chews your walls, doors, etc.

FredaHogan

HOW TO STOP YOUR DOG FROM CHEWING WOOD FITTINGS IN THE HOUSE WHEN SPRINKLING BLACK PEPPER DOESN'T WORK

Sprinkle the wood with Tabasco sauce—it's very, very hot. Did this for our Staffordshire terrier when he was a puppy and he stopped after the first chew.

toptiptwin

HOW TO STOP YOUR DOG FROM LICKING THE INCISION
AFTER AN OPERATION

My vet suggested putting a T-shirt on my dog. You put it on like you would on a person. She seemed happy with it and didn't lick the wound.

Nico

HOW TO STOP YOUR DOG FROM JUMPING UP AT GUESTS

Tell your guests to completely ignore the dog. Don't even look at it. It will then get less excited and shut up.

pgrier

HOW TO GET YOUR HORSE TO TRUST YOU MORE

Here is an exercise to build trust between horse and owner. First, put the horse in a school and go with him. Take off the halter and lead and chase him off. Make him run circles around the pen until you see certain signs: his inside ear pointing toward the center of the ring where you are standing and chewing movements with his mouth. Now stop chasing him and turn away. Wait until he walks to you. Make him follow you, then reward him.

soccerchic99

HOW TO KEEP YOUR PONY'S MANE AND TAIL CLEAN AND TANGLE FREE

After washing the mane or tail, thoroughly brush in cheap furniture polish. This not only keeps it tangle free but also protects the hair from dirt. I find it easier to spray the polish onto the brush and then brush the mane/tail. Repeat until all the hair is coated.

HDC1960

HOW TO SAVE TIME IN STABLES ON A WEEKDAY

On the weekend, when you have more time, fill enough hay nets to last the week. I fill seven, one for each day, but if my horse is kept in due to bad weather I have to fill the odd one during the week.

Make up enough dry feeds for the week and put into plastic bags.

If you use sugar beet pulp, soak enough for the week—it will keep well in cold weather.

I muck out on the weekend, Tuesday, and Thursday. It takes me only about an hour to muck out and mix feeds during the week.

I don't groom during the week, only picking out his feet if required.

edfin

I have a small grooming kit in a trug type of bucket in the stable corner—just a couple of brushes and a hoof pick for quick flicks and a bottle of fly repellent for a quick spray. Across two of the rafters I have tied baling twine so it hangs down at the back of the stable about three yards apart. I have slipped a strong drainpipe through the tied twine and I use this to hang rugs on, saving the walk to the tack room. Keep everything as close at hand as possible.

COLIYTYHE

HOW TO GET RID OF GREEN ALGAE IN YOUR RABBIT'S WATER BOTTLES

Use products for sterilizing babies' bottles and rinse out well.

Bumpy

HOW TO KEEP RABBITS COOL

I put a bottle of frozen water in a big sock and they lie next to it when they need to be cooled down. Make sure their hutch/run has plenty of shade. If they drink from a bowl, you can put a couple of ice cubes in the water.

femme_fatale

Relationships

or All he knows about me is that I'm a good listener.

I have always been profoundly grateful for being set up on dates, but there have been one or two that were categorically a waste of makeup. As one of our Top Tipsters, LindaCee, says in this chapter, watch out for the self-absorbed ones who talk only about themselves. But although babbling on and on is unforgivable, it is understandable—it's symptomatic of the desire to be known, a great human need. Which is why it is so enraging to spend a four-hour date learning everything about him, his career, his divorce, his children, his siblings, his parents, his parents' divorce, and his dog when he asks not a single question about you, and still thinks you're going to sleep with him—because you have such a great "connection."

WHY THE GUYS WE LIKE NEVER CALL

There are tons of reasons: He's not into you, he doesn't know you're into him, you're not emotionally available, he's not looking for a relationship . . . the list is endless. But be reassured, the one who's supposed to call always does.

telladore

HOW TO CHOOSE BETWEEN TWO MEN

Imagine your life six months, two years, and ten years from now. Assess which man you'd rather be with in each stage of your life. Whoever you see in two or even all three stages of your life, keep.

DezG

Look at each man's father, assess which one has aged better and how he treats his wife, then choose the man with the best dad.

BooBoo

A friend once told me, "Learn to fancy the nice ones—they will make you happy." Stupidly, I never learned that lesson and as a forty-year-old I am still single (and childless, gulp) because I never fancied the guys who would actually be kind and nice to me. Learn from my mistakes!

twink

HOW TO DEAL WITH A MAN WHO SEEMS TOO CAREFUL
WITH MONEY

How to deal with him? Accept this part of him, because he will not change. Financial habits rarely change. Don't think that anything you do will change his behavior and don't even try unless you enjoy knocking your head against a brick wall. Financial compatibility is one of the key areas that couples should explore completely before marriage. It's a real relationship killer.

sandrasimmons

HOW TO FIND A RICH GUY

The trouble with looking for a rich guy is that rich guys have radar for women like that. They will certainly sleep with you, may well go out with you, but if they know you're after their money they certainly won't marry you. They didn't get rich by being dumb. There's an old saying—If you marry for money, you earn it twice over. Why don't you just make your own money and look for companionship, humor, and love in a man?

Willa

HOW TO GET RID OF A MAN WHO BLACKMAILS YOU OVER A NAKED PICTURE HE HAS OF YOU

It's against the law for him to publish photos of that nature without your permission, even if it's just something he sends as a text message, so threaten him with the police. Even if you're bluffing, the threat may be enough to get rid of him. If you're young and scared that he will show your parents, tell them first. They may be shocked that you were naive enough to allow yourself to be photographed by this pathetic pervert, but I'm sure they're already aware that you were in an intimate relationship with him and will provide you with the support you so badly need.

LindaCee

HOW TO KNOW IF HE LIKES YOU

One word: effort. Does he make an effort to be with you or talk to you? Then he's into you.

Jillaroo95

HOW TO LOVE

The only answer to this is to love someone as you would want to be loved.

Carissa

HOW TO SLEEP NEXT TO A GUY IN A SEXY WAY

The sexiest thing my man said to me in the first month of dating: "As much as I love you getting dressed up to the nines and looking glamorous, the most intimate boost to my ego is seeing you first thing in the morning, no makeup, bleary eyes the morning after, because no one else gets that chance to wake up with you but me."

Yeah, I love him.

heroinegirl

HOW TO STOP MY BOYFRIEND FROM CRITICIZING ME—MY CHOICE OF CLOTHES, LACK OF A TAN, DRINKING TOO MUCH, MY FAMILY, AND MY FRIENDS

The perfect way to make sure he stops criticizing everything about you is to dump him!

MenopausalMadam

HOW TO KNOW IF IT'S NORMAL TO HAVE DOUBTS IN A RELATIONSHIP

You'll never find the perfect house in the perfect street, facing the right way with the right number of bedrooms. Everything is a compromise and you have to be flexible and adaptable. It can be worked out if you want it to be. It is up to you.

operatix

WHAT TO DO IF HE DOESN'T REPLY TO YOUR
TEXT MESSAGE

Do nothing! Respect his privacy. He may be busy or he may be ignoring you. You'll never know if you send another text. The second text will only annoy him. And never let him know that you wasted a single second waiting for a reply.

Masi

HOW TO SUCCESSFULLY ARGUE YOUR POINT WITH
YOUR BOYFRIEND

If he's drunk, wait until he's sober. If he's tired, wait until he's had some sleep. If he's hungry, wait until he's had some food. If he's generally in a bad mood, just leave him alone until he feels better. Be calm and don't raise your voice. If he talks back, just listen to what he has to say, no matter how stupid it might be. Show him that you heard him ("I understand that you didn't do that on purpose, but . . ."). Suggest a precise so-lution ("You need to start to treat me better/be a better man" is not a good one). If it has anything to do with emotions or "girly" things, put it in very simple words. ("When I put on a dress, it means I want you to tell me I'm beautiful.")

gnrbu

HOW TO MAKE YOUR BOYFRIEND MORE CARING

There's a very wise and true saying: "The only thing a woman has ever been able to change about a man is his diapers." If he's not a caring kind of guy, you aren't going to be able to change that. However, you can tell him what you like and what is important to you. If he truly cares about your feelings he will make the effort.

Jillaroo95

WHAT TO DO WHEN YOUR BOYFRIEND EYES OTHER WOMEN

Distract him by making nonsexual observations about the woman he is eyeing like, "That girl has really pretty hair" or "great jacket." That tells him you notice he is looking and brings the attention back to you.

WooHoo

You can't stop him from looking at other girls any more than he can stop you from shopping for shoes you don't need, or spending two hours trying to decide what to wear, only to change your mind for the fiftieth time at the last minute.

It all comes down to understanding each other. To be honest, he probably doesn't even realize he's looking; it's just one of those built-in automatic reflex reactions in guys.

If, however, he starts comparing you with these other girls, the best way to stop him from looking at them is to gouge his eyes out with an ice cream scoop. . . .

Binny

HOW CAN I END MY RELATIONSHIP WITH MY YOUNG SON'S FATHER WITHOUT IT HURTING MY SON

Never, ever speak ill of his father to your son. If your son ever tells you that his dad says bad things about you, tell him that his daddy is feeling unhappy, and that if he (the son) tells his father that he loves him, it will help. Tell him that no matter how his father feels about you, he loves the son. If the father is a total pill, your son will figure it out on his own when he's older, and you will have taken the high road.

asildem

HOW TO END AN UNHEALTHY RELATIONSHIP

Have a good think about why you've stayed with him so far. Are you so horrible a person that he's all you deserve? Do your friends think about you in that way? I bet they don't. Talk to your friends about why you feel you deserve this treatment. Whether you accept it or not, you definitely deserve better and will probably look back on this episode and wonder what on earth you were thinking to stay with him as long as you did!

TizzysMum

Here is a good mantra for life, not just men, that I often give to my divorce clients: "You can only—ever—control your own actions, not those of anybody else, so don't waste your time trying." This man will mistreat you as long as you let him, so stop letting him.

corkychum

HOW TO GET MY BOYFRIEND TO LET ME GO

You are the one who has to make the decision to move on. Don't give him the power or control; this is *your* decision. Presuming he's not a stalker and doesn't have you tied up in a basement somewhere (with a copy of this book, of course), all you have to do is walk away and don't look back. A clean break is often the easiest: don't talk, call, text, etc. That way he has less opportunity to lure you back with a guilt trip (and no great romance is ever based on guilt). It's not unusual to feel bad when breaking up with someone, especially if he's nice and you've just grown apart. But it is unhealthy to stay in a relationship that you know is not working. Set *yourself* free.

DezG

HOW TO GET OVER BEING DUMPED BY YOUR HUSBAND
OF MANY YEARS

Tell yourself that you are moving on to a new phase of your life, one that is open to many possibilities. (I know this is hard now, but it will get easier as time goes on. In the meantime, make it your mantra.) You have the chance to redefine who you are and live your life on *your* terms. You might also want to concentrate on those things your husband did that got on your nerves and be thankful you no longer have to deal with them.

Jillaroo95

HOW TO REALLY BELIEVE "I'M WORTH MORE THAN THIS" WHEN A MAN IS NOT TREATING YOU WELL

Ask yourself, very seriously, what you would think/feel/say if your best friend had such a relationship. Your sister? Your daughter? Are you worth less than these people?

Jennynib

HOW TO STOP THE FEAR OF BEING ALONE AFTER A LONG RELATIONSHIP

I suffered from loneliness very badly after my marriage ended. I found myself standing in the street sometimes, unsure which way to turn as I didn't know what I liked anymore, only what "we" liked. That is the key thing: You have to get to know yourself again. Try and remember what you liked to do before the relationship. Take up an old or new hobby. Buy something frivolous. Invite your friends over. Watch trashy TV that will make you laugh. Find mechanisms that take you out of your slump when you feel the fear coming on. Being alone doesn't have to mean lonely. You'll find a new independence and a lust for the single life again.

DeeDee73

HOW TO GET OVER THE GUILT OF CHEATING ON YOUR PARTNER

Folks who get over the guilt of cheating often cheat again. I'd recommend some sort of atonement for cheating, so that you may eventually forgive yourself but don't lose that guilt completely. Feeling guilty about something like cheating is what makes you a good human and not a sociopath.

Jillaroo95

HOW TO KNOW IF HE IS CHEATING ON YOU

I love the female species, because we have special things like intuition. I was OK around my partner until about six months into our relationship; suddenly I was acting "paranoid." We women are not paranoid; we just know what's going on, but can't put our finger on it. My ex stopped having sex, always went out on weekends, had his phone glued to his hand, and even went to the bathroom with it! He stopped texting me, yet his phone bill was always huge. He always name-dropped, saying "it's just Mark" when texts were coming every two minutes (even at 4 a.m.!). Stopped giving me a kiss when coming home from work and went straight into the shower, probably to wash off his lady smell.

BooBoo

Mine started wearing purple silk boxer shorts. I can only assume it is a ritual for guys afflicted with Wandering Willy syndrome . . . a need (if you will) to decorate the appendage in imperial purple. By the way, I found that placing a hidden voice-activated dictation machine within the confines of the car offered a good deal of information.

ladydigger

WHAT TO DO IF YOU KNOW YOUR BOYFRIEND IS A CHEATER BUT CANNOT TELL HIM YOU FOUND OUT, PLUS HOW TO GET REVENGE AND MOVE ON

Be classy. You don't have to tell him you know he was cheating on you in order to get revenge; in fact, the most effective way of hurting him would be to dump him on the pretense that he's too dull/you're just not very attracted to him anymore/ you don't think he's real long-term-partner potential. While he knows he's a cheating scumbag, he'll also think that you're dumping him for the simple reason that in some way he is completely inadequate—thus making you look smarter than you would if you confronted him about it and had an argument before splitting.

caterianne

HOW TO RESPOND TO AN ANONYMOUS TEXT SAYING
YOUR BOYFRIEND IS CHEATING, AND HE DENIES IT

Get *him* to call the number back, in front of you. (Especially if he does it from his phone.) If he cares about you there's no way he could back out of it.

Tooke

HOW TO ASK THE FRIEND YOU HAVE BEEN SLEEPING
WITH FOR A COMMITMENT

You aren't friends. Friends don't sleep together; friends go out for coffee, chill out together, etc., but they don't have sex!

I would back away from him and not make contact; wait for him to contact you. That will give you the opportunity to tell him what you want out of the relationship. If he doesn't want the same thing and only wants the convenience of sleeping with you with no emotional ties, let him go—you are worth *far* more than that. Only sleep with someone who is committed to you; don't give yourself away for nothing.

DOZIGGY

HOW TO GET YOUR BOYFRIEND TO COMMIT

Some men just aren't the commitment kind, and there's nothing you can do to change it. Some realize too late (i.e., after the wedding) that they aren't up for it. Just make sure there are fabulous, happy bits of your life that don't include him. If he wants more (but not all!) of your attention, he'll have to make it worth your while by committing. If he doesn't want you to be committed to him, you should stop wasting your time and move on.

tiptoetipster

HOW TO HAVE A RELATIONSHIP WITH A COMMITMENT-PHOBIC MAN

Go for it, if you don't think you deserve any better and enjoy hard work with very little reward. Seriously, some women go for men like this because subconsciously they themselves don't want to be tied down.

LindaCee

HOW TO FIND GREAT TOPICS OF CONVERSATION WITH YOUR BOYFRIEND

Take up a new hobby together—the more outlandish the better. That will give you a host of things to talk about.

Jillaroo95

HOW TO GET HIM TO TALK MORE

Go for long drives. Men seem to talk more when sitting shoulder-to-shoulder rather than face to face. I think they get intimidated by the eye-contact thing. Steer the conversation away from relationships on the first few drives.

Masi

HOW TO MAKE A MAN LISTEN TO YOU

Go over to the television, switch it off, stand in front of it, and say what you want to say!

MenopausalMadam

HOW TO MAKE A MESSY MAN INTO
A HOUSE-PROUD MAN

Frame this as a problem-solving exercise; guys tend to tackle things this way. For instance, ask him to figure out the most efficient way to clean something. Or turn it into a competition, as in, "I can do this faster than you."

Jillaroo95

HOW TO ENCOURAGE YOUR BOYFRIEND TO CLEAN
MORE OFTEN

Make a boyfriend box. Use a storage box and tell him that you are going to fill it with any of his things that you find out of place. If he doesn't reclaim them by the time the box is full, you will sell/donate/throw away the contents of the box.

LittleMissSunshine

HOW TO ASK A GUY OUT

You can always buy tickets for a concert or cinema and then invite him, telling him you've been given the tickets. Or have a few friends over for drinks or supper and invite him, too.

operatix

HOW TO BE APPROACHABLE

When you're out with a group of girls, you may find no guy will come up to you. Men are frightened of a group! If you are out with your girlfriends, once in a while head to the bar on your own to "get drinks." He may well come right over!

lauricha

HOW TO CHAT UP A MAN

Try meeting a guy's eyes and smiling at him—it really is that simple. If he's interested, the encouragement will prompt him to come over and chat with you.

Jillaroo95

HOW TO GET TO KNOW EACH OTHER ON A FIRST DATE

The best first date I've heard about was when my best friend was taken to the local amusement park. She said it was brilliant because they were busy doing things and having fun, and it took away the nerves and awkward silences. Bowling, while cheesy, has the same effect. The movies are a definite no no—how can you get to know someone sitting in the dark in silence?

Emu80

HOW TO JUDGE A FIRST DATE

My main test after a first date is to ask myself how much he's discovered about me and how much I've learned about him. I went out with a guy the other week and in the space of two hours I heard about his schooling, his marriage, his divorce, his kids, his *parents'* divorce (for God's sake!), his job, his plans for the future . . . I literally couldn't get a word in edgewise, so all he learned about me is that I'm a good listener.

In other words, my advice is just to be interested in him and ask him about his life. There's nothing more attractive than someone actually wanting to know about your thoughts and opinions, but also learn to watch out for the selfish beggars.

LindaCee

HOW TO DEAL WITH A GUY WHO'S PROMISED TO BREAK UP WITH HIS GIRLFRIEND TO BE WITH YOU BUT NEVER DOES

I don't mean to sound harsh, but he isn't going to leave her. If he really wanted to, he would have done it already. He just wants his bread buttered on both sides. Besides, what's to say he won't do the same thing to you?

rencha

HOW TO FIND OUT IF A MAN IS MARRIED AND HASN'T TOLD YOU

Listen to your inner voice and what it is telling you. Other signs: He has a white tan line on his ring finger, he won't give you his home phone number, he doesn't introduce you to family members or close friends, he cancels dates often and at the last minute, he is never available for overnights or weekends away, and he never talks about his home life. Just a few thoughts.

ashling

HOW TO GET OUT OF A DATE WITH SOMEONE YOU FIND
VERY UNATTRACTIVE WITHOUT HURTING HIM

Tell him you've been dating someone recently, but it's becoming more serious and you don't think it's appropriate for you to be dating anyone else. "Sorry to let you down, but I did think it was important to be honest with you." It's a lie, but it will do the trick without making him feel awful.

LindaCee

HOW TO REFUSE A DATE WHEN YOU ARE NOT INTERESTED

Start with a straight "Thanks for asking, but I don't think so," because you really don't need to make excuses for yourself. If he asks why, tell him, "I just don't think we're suited in that way." If he starts to go on about really liking you, say, "I appreciate that, but I don't feel the same way, so let's leave it there, shall we?" You need to retain control of these conversations. Be firm but polite and don't think you have to put up with the guy badgering you. It's not your problem if he refuses to hear the word *no*.

LindaCee

HOW TO STOP BEING SCARED OF DATING

Pretty much everyone is nervous when it comes to dating. Try to look on it as an adventure—tell yourself that it's exciting, not scary.

Jillaroo95

HOW TO ACT AROUND YOUR EX WHEN YOU ARE STILL FRIENDS BUT HE IS FINDING IT HARD TO MOVE ON

Why are you still friends when he is heartbroken? You think what you are doing is helpful and comforting, but it's really the opposite. Being friends with an ex at this stage is more work than being in an actual relationship. You have to conform to his needs, worry about how he's doing, and hide your true feelings while trying to comfort him as a "friend." When you said goodbye to him, you said goodbye to cuddling, hanging out, support, *and* friendship. You and your ex are just holding on to something you may or may not have realized you were giving up. You have to realize that when a relationship is over, the perks of being a friend are over. You have to go cold turkey, at least until *both* of you are over it and want to be friends again.

lazzykittyy

HOW TO ACT WHEN YOU FIND DIRTY TEXTS, PHOTOS, AND VIDEOS SENT TO YOUR BOYFRIEND'S PHONE FROM HIS STALKER EX

You need to make it *very, very* clear to your boyfriend that you will not be happy if he continues regular contact with this nutcase. His ego is currently getting a good old massage and he's only going to cut ties with her when it hits home what he risks losing.

I've no doubt she means absolutely nothing to him, but he must feel like sex on legs at the moment, and what man is going to knock that back until he's forced to?

TizzysMum

HOW TO DEAL WITH AN EX WHO SAYS HE MISSES YOU, BUT HASN'T MENTIONED HIS NEW GIRLFRIEND, WHOM YOU KNOW ALL ABOUT

Tell him you miss him too and that you were only saying that last night to your new boyfriend . . .

ladydigger

HOW TO DEAL WITH FINDING NAKED PHOTOS OF YOUR PARTNER'S EX-WIFE AMONG HIS BELONGINGS

Don't you have old love letters? A few photos of your exes? Yearbooks with hearts drawn around the boys you liked? All of those things can be less shocking than naked photos but they all mean the same thing: We like to document our history. Those naked photos are a part of you partner's past. Stop looking through his stuff (yes, we all deserve to have something private).

stelladore

HOW TO DEAL WITH YOUR EX TAKING THE KIDS OUT FOR THE DAY WITH HIS NEW GIRLFRIEND

Accept that your ex was always going to meet someone new at some point and, providing you trust him to look after your kids properly, look on these excursions as an opportunity for you to have some grown-up time for yourself. Arrange to see your friends, go for a beauty treatment, go clothes shopping, go to the movies (and see something noncartoonish!), or, when you're a little more chilled about the situation and don't need the distraction, just enjoy a little time alone. I'm sure you agree that your ex has every right to see his kids, and his present/ future girlfriends will never mean anything to them in comparison to you, so spin something positive out of these occasions.

Elsie

HOW TO GET OVER AN EX

Treat yourself like a recovering addict—you are addicted to this man and you need to wean yourself off him. You can only take things one day at a time. Say to yourself, "For today I will not contact him."

Tooke

Other than through a lobotomy or a stroke? Sorry to say, there is no magic process to help you forget something. However, you can transmute the memory. Keep in mind that humans learn more from mistakes than successes. If you want to forget something bad that happened, whenever you think of it, immediately think of a lesson you learned or could learn from it. You won't forget the incident, but the accompanying feelings and thoughts about it will adjust over time.

Jillaroo95

HOW TO GET RID OF A VERY ANNOYING, PESTERING EX-LOVER

Some guys can be quite creative with their state of denial. I once had a guy who could not understand that I meant it when I tried to tell him nicely that it was over. He came up with bizarre reasons like maybe I couldn't have kids (I can, BTW) and didn't want to drag him into it, so I lost my patience and told him, "I will never, ever fall in love with you. I want to be with someone that I *want*, and that's not you. Frankly, the fact that you can't even see that, despite my many attempts to get the message across to you nicely, means that you're so focused on yourself you don't actually know what it means to care about what I'm feeling. It's over." Worked like magic.

jjj

HOW TO BEHAVE WHEN YOU REALLY LIKE YOUR (MALE) BEST FRIEND BUT ARE SCARED OF RUINING THE FRIENDSHIP BY COMING ON TO HIM

This is going to sound patronizing, but I think it depends a bit on how old you both are. When older people (who have been around the block a few times!) get together with a friend, it can be hugely successful. Both parties know what they are getting into and have usually weighed the consequences.

It's just harder when you are young. Younger men don't always think with their hearts and heads about these things. He may respond if you come on to him physically and then feel embarrassed and regretful later. Also, in your teens and early twenties, a male friend is *such* a gift . . . so much insight into the male psyche, friends of his own to introduce you to—the list goes on and on. I'd avoid making a move if you can bear it—you have a lot to lose.

Rosebudsmummy

HOW TO MEET A PARTNER ON THE INTERNET

That's how I met Jack—and we just celebrated our sixth anniversary. The fact is, you'll meet a variety of men this way; some will be unsuitable and some will be quite nice. First, look at your own profile and make sure that the picture is current, isn't of you in a bikini or otherwise skimpily clad, and that your profile text is as honest as possible—your profile should reflect the real you, not the person you want to be. And state what you are looking for without going into what you don't want (that will make you sound too bitter.) Then, take a close look at the men's profiles to check for clichés and such and if necessary, have your most honest and forthright friends read them and give you their opinions.

Jillaroo95

HOW TO BE GRACIOUS WHEN YOUR HUSBAND MAKES NO EFFORT FOR YOUR FIRST WEDDING ANNIVERSARY

Tease him about it. This way you can get your point across without any aggravation. He will be feeling guilty anyway. Teasing and joking is usually the best way to deal with any grievances. There's no point in being bad-tempered!

operatix

HOW TO KEEP A RELATIONSHIP HAPPY AFTER THE BIRTH OF A BABY

Take time to talk to each other—over dinner, face-to-face, and ask how he is, how he is finding the new routine—and remain interested in his work and what he does all day. Though it might be the last thing on your mind, your love life is vitally important too. So mentally put aside time for romance: I say mentally, because at this stage spontaneity doesn't come naturally, so, without telling him, add it to the routine you are probably doggedly following (awful as this sounds, it does make it easier to schedule romance along with everything else!). Even better, do something special for him on a weeknight, when he's least expecting it.

Abi1973

Don't forget each other, as you'll both be showing massive amounts of adoration to the new arrival and either partner can get jealous of that. Make sure you say, "Thank you for my baby," so your partner knows he's responsible for your happiness.

Esme

HOW TO GET OVER THE FACT THAT YOU HAVE TO SHARE YOUR PARTNER WITH HIS EX AND THEIR KIDS

You don't have to. No one is forced to do/accept anything they don't like. We all have a choice. What I am going to tell you now is the best advice that I have been given, and it really worked for me:

Make a decision.

Stick to it.

Don't look back.

milou

HOW TO DISCIPLINE YOUR BOYFRIEND'S CHILD WHEN YOU LIVE TOGETHER WITHOUT CAUSING CONFLICT

My advice would be to leave the disciplining to your boyfriend and not get involved. However, that doesn't mean accepting bad behavior. When he or she is behaving badly, gently point it out to your boyfriend for him to sort out. Men are generally unaware, so a gentle, "Jimmy is peeing in the sink, can you talk to him?" will prompt him to deal with it. Build the relationship with the child slowly. My daughter adores her stepfather but he took it slowly and sat back and let her learn to love him.

Ermentrude

HOW TO FACE SOMEBODY EVERY DAY WHO HAS TURNED YOU DOWN WITHOUT FEELING UTTERLY AWFUL

Turn it around—if a guy you didn't like asked you out and you turned him down, would you expect him to avoid you? I doubt it. I'm sure he's also slightly embarrassed, but honestly, the best thing you can do is brazen it out. Smile and say good morning next time you see him and get on with your day.

I had a similar situation on the night my friend met her boyfriend. I had a bit of a drunken kiss with his friend, despite him being twenty-eight and me being . . . well . . . forty plus, shall we say? Then she and the boyfriend got serious and I was introduced to the young one again—stone cold sober! All I could do was make a joke of it in a "oh yeah, I vaguely remember you!" kind of way. The less fuss you make, the sooner these mortifying feelings will disappear.

Elsie

HOW TO KEEP A RELATIONSHIP INTERESTING AND EXCITING

1. Write him notes and stick them in places he'll find them when you're not there.
2. Establish a fortnightly date night, where you alternate who chooses the restaurant/movie and keep it a surprise until you get there.
3. Find fun things you can do together, ideally in the com-

fort of your own home (where you're most likely to stick to them!). This means anything from inventing your own cocktails and naming them to playing Monopoly.

4. Give each other space! There's no way to kill the romance like spending too much time together. Just think, if you only spent time together, you'd never have any funny stories to share.

5. Keep the passion by surprising each other. Think massages, naked Twister, chocolate sauce fights, or whatever. Just remember to keep things spontaneous.

caterianne

HOW TO ASK YOUR BOYFRIEND WHEN YOU WANT SEX

Depends on the guy; here are a few suggestions:

1. Use the stealth mode (guys use this a lot). Start out by giving him a backrub or otherwise caressing him and end up with your hands under his shirt, progressing from there. He'll get the message.

2. Bring it up in a flirty/joking way. This will break the ice and make you both more comfortable.

3. Be direct, as in "I'd really like to _____."

4. Grab him by the lapels and throw him on the bed or other horizontal surface. Unless he has power issues, he'll be extremely flattered and turned on.

Jillaroo95

General rules for a successful good time in the sack include the following:

Be relaxed.

Make him laugh (try a seductive dance wearing only his socks and a hand towel!).

Never discuss your past amours in bed.

Feel great about your body. He already feels that way about your body; otherwise you would not be in bed in the first place. Your personal confidence will make you feel and look fabulous.

Treat his body like an adventure. Tell him how attractive he is.

In short, massage the body *and* the ego and he will be gagging for more.

ladydigger

Stop watching movie sex—it's not real! The real thing is silly and messy and fun and not perfect every time. So one day it might be great, the next, for whatever reason, just OK. Show willingness, it's a real turn-on. Don't put pressure on yourself to try a million different things because you're worried the missionary position is boring; just ask what he likes and say what you'd like in return! Now, stop reading this and go practice, practice, practice!

DeeDee73

Never fake an orgasm! First of all, it's lying to your partner, and if your relationship is more than just rolling in the hay that's never a good idea. Second, if you respond favorably to something that he's doing, he'll likely keep doing it, so you're encouraging him to do whatever random not-good thing he happens to be doing at the time.

guamae

HOW TO ACT WHEN YOU REALLY LIKE THE GUY YOU'RE DATING—EXCEPT FOR THE WAY HE KISSES

Several ways—you can either stick to your guns and hope he adjusts to you, or you adjust to him. Guys love it if you say they're good at something—it boosts their self-esteem—but be subtle and say, "I love the way you kiss but you know it turns me on more if you . . ." (describe how you want him to do it). If he knows he's satisfying you, he will do it more.

BooBoo

HOW TO KNOW IF YOUR DATE JUST WANTS SEX

Suggest going out on a proper date. If he says something like, "I'd rather come to your place to watch a DVD or something," feel free to interpret that as "I have no intention of spending any money on you, having my friends see me with you, or listening to you any more than I have to—I just want to have sex with you."

TizzysMum

HOW TO KISS (A TIP FOR MEN)

Just occasionally, enjoy kissing for its own sake and don't assume that it's a prelude to sex. There's nothing more tiresome than being mid-makeout and just *knowing* that he is, without fail, going to make a grab for your boob.

LindaCee

Safety

or If you can't be good, be careful.

Much of our personal safety is common sense, and what isn't is largely beyond our control. You can lock your doors at night, never get into cars with strangers, and avoid dimly lit alleyways as though your life depends on it (which indeed it does), but there is little you can do if some moron decides to drink and drive, or your neighborhood psycho is convinced that you're his mother. The only thing you can do is to arm yourself with a highly developed sense of self-preservation and learn enough self-defense maneuvers to see off all but the most dogged of creeps. Luckily, the unmistakable sound of an ax-wielding maniac stumbling around your kitchen in the middle of the night will almost always be a figment of your imagination.

HOW TO BE SAFE

Be proactive. If you are walking alone, always know where your cell phone and keys are so you are prepared. Be confident and walk briskly. Predators tend to prey on easy targets; if you are walking fast and seem strong and confident, you are less of a target. Also, eye contact and saying hello is off-putting. I work late and have to park down the street from my building. Whenever I see someone approaching I look him directly in the eye and say hello very firmly. That way he knows I mean business. If someone is following you or you sense someone might be following you, stop in a well lit and preferably busy area and let him pass. Watch until he's far enough away and then continue with your walk.

Melie

When you're out and about, always be aware of who's around you on the street. Don't walk with your head down, texting with your handbag dangling off one arm. A man tried to mug me once when I was taking money out of an ATM (in broad daylight on a busy street!). He put his arm around my neck and I reacted by launching myself backwards, turning around, pushing him away from me, and roaring straight into his face like a lion. (Thank you, Oprah!) It scared the bejesus out of him.

guineapig

HOW TO GUARD YOUR HANDBAG

Best of all is to use a bag with a zipper and a long strap you can sling diagonally across your body, so nothing can be removed surreptitiously. If it has a shorter handle, when you are sitting down (in a restaurant or toilet) you can leave your handbag on the floor between both feet with the handle/strap around your ankle (or the leg of your chair). Just be sure to unhook it and pick it up before you stand up!

Abi1973

HOW TO BE SAFE WHEN MEETING IN PERSON SOMEONE
YOU HAVE MET ON THE INTERNET

Meet in a public place, tell someone where you are going, and ask that person to call you if they haven't heard from you by a certain time. Or go with someone to meet this person. Make sure you stay on neutral ground and if you feel uncomfortable, *leave*!

harriet1

Don't tell him where you live or arrange for him to pick you up at your house. Don't give him your phone number; take his.

guineapig

HOW TO EVADE A GUN-TOTING MANIAC

If the predator has a gun and you are not under his control, even though it seems scary, *always* run! The predator will hit you (a running target) only four in one hundred times; and even then, it most likely will not be a vital organ. *Run!*

toobesr

HOW TO DETER BURGLARS

Experiment with lights to leave on while you are out. Go and stand in the street and look critically at your house. Does it look as though someone is at home? Choose some curtains to leave mostly drawn and lamps on so that it looks as though you are in, but upstairs.

Rosebudsmummy

If your garden comes close to your downstairs window, plant prickly shrubs. You can get pretty flowering ones with spiky stems and leaves. That will help. If not, perhaps you can plant window boxes, which will deter burglars as being too much effort to get past and draw attention to any attempt at a break-in. They will find an easier home to try.

ashling

HOW TO SECURE YOUR HOUSE WHILE YOU'RE AWAY

Make sure you cancel any deliveries such as newspapers, as these can pile up and advertise an empty house. Double-check your locks and be sure your house insurance is up to date, with any new or expensive items included in your policy. Get some timers for your lights and sockets, and set a radio or television to come on at random intervals. Ask a friend to check on your home while you're away, and leave contact numbers for any emergency.

Noreen

HOW TO AVOID BEING CAR-JACKED

Be aware of a car-jacking ploy: You unlock your car and get inside. Then you lock all your doors, start the engine, and shift into reverse. You look into the rear-view mirror to back out of your parking space and notice a piece of paper stuck to the middle of the rear window. So you shift back into park or neutral, unlock your doors and jump out of your car to remove that paper or whatever it is that is obstructing your view. When you reach the back of your car, the car-jacker appears out of nowhere, jumps in, and takes off.

BooBoo

HOW TO BE SAFE IN A PARKING LOT

Women have a tendency to get into their cars and just sit (getting organized, doing their checkbook, or making a list). Don't do this! A predator could be watching you, and this is the perfect opportunity for him to get in on the passenger side. As soon as you get into your car, lock the doors and drive away.

Tooke

HOW TO COPE WITH A MUGGER

If a robber demands your handbag, do not hand it to him; toss it away from you instead. He is probably more interested in your handbag than in you and he will go for the handbag. Run like mad in the other direction.

pingle

HOW TO DEFEND YOURSELF

The little finger is weak, so if someone grabs hold of you go for his little finger and pull like hell; the rest of the hand has to follow. Act quickly though, before he has time to think what you're doing. Eyes make a good target too, so stick your fingers in. And give the top lip a good hard twist. The solar plexus is also a good place to hit if you're being attacked; that'll wind him. A hard shoe sole run down a shin will hurt, as will a poke from a couple of fingers into the base of the throat. Don't worry about hurting a would-be attacker—self-preservation first.

COLIYTYHE

HOW TO MAKE SURE YOUR CHILD IS AS SAFE AS POSSIBLE WHILE TRAVELING

Buy them a large door wedge to pack with them and tell them to use it every night. This is also good for students sharing houses who don't want unwelcome advances in the night.

patsharp

If he is trustworthy, give him a credit card to be used in emergencies only. Motivate him not to use it frivolously by saying you'll give him a certain amount of money when he gets home if it's unused.

Gia

Agree that she will call or email you, just to check in, every forty-eight hours or so. Ask her to give you a copy of her itinerary and to let you know if she decides to make any changes. Although she is no doubt longing to spread her wings, she's probably a bit scared, too.

Orinda

HOW TO SLEEP SOUNDLY WHEN TRAVELING ALONE

Always check the evacuation routes as soon as you get to the room, so you won't panic if there is an emergency. Count alcoves/doors so you can find your way in the dark.

For security, if there isn't a chair to jam under the door handle, use items in the room to "booby trap" the area by the door and window—glasses, snacks from the minibar, etc.— anything noisy and/or breakable.

villanova

HOW TO CALL THE EMERGENCY NUMBER ANYWHERE

Most cell phones are preprogrammed with the three international emergency numbers (911, 999, and 112). The phone will use any nearby signal and even works when the keypad is locked.

Ruth

School

or If you survive unscathed, office politics will be a walk in the park.

*I*f life is an attempt to keep the tidal wave of disorder and chaos at bay, school is not helpful. It only adds to the challenge. The days of the single school bag containing an apple, a pair of sneakers, and a physics textbook are long gone. Today's children have book backpacks (usually available for only $50 from the school itself); to this must be added a flute bag, a packed lunch, sports kit, swimming kit, and at least one costume for the next play or mime evening. It's an iron law of the universe that at least one of those bags will go into a worm hole in the space-time continuum between the front door and school. You may think there is something to be said for the Spartan system when parenting was shared by a pool of parents with everyone pitching in. However, no Spartan was ever given a handmade birthday card by her four-year-old. And so we continue with this elaborate caretaking until they are eighteen, as a way of allowing young people to learn about the stuff we're too embarrassed to tell them, like smoking and drinking and sex.

HOW TO HELP CHILDREN FEEL MORE COMFORTABLE ON THEIR FIRST DAY OF SCHOOL

Contact parents of children in the same class and arrange a playdate before school starts so your child sees some familiar faces when he/she first enters the classroom. If the school will not give out that information, you could ask them to offer the invitation on your behalf.

Ruth

Make sure they have a map of the school to look at and talk about it with them. They can see where they have assembly, where they play, and where they have lessons. It will make the whole school seem less intimidating and help them understand how the school works.

Wex

HOW TO ADVISE YOUR DAUGHTER IF SHE'S BEING CALLED A SNOB AT SCHOOL

Tell her it's easy to believe that everyone else is doing what you're not, like drinking, sleeping with lots of boys, and doing drugs, but they're not—a lot of what people say is bravado. Some people don't have the strength to stand apart from the crowd, and they just follow their peers like sheep, desperate to fit in. But there will always be people like you who want to follow your own rules, and that's great! Just a word of warning though—try not to look down your nose at people who don't reflect your own values. If you adopt a "this is what I like to do, and that is what you like to do, and it's no big deal that we're different" attitude, you won't go far wrong.

LindaCee

HOW TO HELP YOUR CHILD REPORT A BULLY

Tell your child to keep a diary of exactly what the bully says/does and when, so he or she can back up what they're saying. It shows that this isn't something petty and will instill confidence when they come to report it. Get them to email their teacher. It may be that during the day the teacher finds it hard to concentrate but if they read it at a quieter time then they have more reason to listen.

FabulousFeminist

HOW TO FOLLOW UP WHEN REPORTING A BULLY TO THE TEACHER HASN'T HELPED

Make a fuss—teachers should stand up for a child who is being bullied and ensure that appropriate action is taken. Does the school have a support network? Visit the school counselor if one is available. I was bullied at school, and telling someone and continuing to tell someone works—kick up a fuss until something is done to stop it.

seagull-pie

HOW TO EARN YOUR OWN MONEY IF YOU'RE STILL IN HIGH SCHOOL

Think outside the box. Talk to the friends of your parents, aunts, uncles, and grandparents; and talk to neighbors to see if they need *anything*—from babysitting to office filing to uploading their CD collection to their iPods. Offer to teach the techie skills high schoolers are famous for to "older" people—how to use a digital camera, how to add numbers to cell phones, how to work iTunes—you'd be surprised how many people could use such lessons!

DezG

HOW TO STUDY WITHOUT GETTING STRESSED-OUT

1. Whenever you finish a topic, write review notes about it. It'll make your life a lot easier when exams come around.
2. If you don't understand something, *don't* put it off. Eventually you'll get swamped with stuff you don't understand. Ask your teacher to sit down and explain it outside of class time.
3. Lots of college students would love to earn some cash

through tutoring. They're cheaper than grown ups, friend-lier, and more flexible timewise.

4. Don't be distracted by friends—try to get as much as possible done during school hours, so when you get home you can have some downtime.

5. Pick one night of the week where you are not allowed to do any homework. It sounds a little odd, but if you know that you can't work on, say, Saturday night, that will prompt you to get your homework done earlier.

caterianne

HOW TO CRAM SUCCESSFULLY FOR AN EXAM IF YOU HAVEN'T LEFT ENOUGH TIME

In general, quickly review the stuff you think you know pretty well, spend more time on the stuff you're less sure of, and, if it really is too late, skip the stuff you never understood. (If you didn't get it in class or on your own the first time, trying to learn it in your few precious moments before the exam is a real long shot.) With any luck, you'll ace the material you know and do well enough on the stuff you spend time reviewing to compensate for the things you never understood.

DezG

A good method is to try and condense a lot of information into a small phrase or word, where each initial stands for some information that is meaningful to the subject. Like the phrase "Richard of York gave battle in vain" to remember the colors of the rainbow. I tried this recently with my exams and was amazed at how much information I could recall from just a seven-letter nonsense word I made up. If the word is funny it's easier to remember.

princess87

HOW TO COPE WITH COLLEGE WORK WHEN YOUR WRITING IS TERRIBLE

Read more. If you're not writing well, it's because you don't know the topic well enough. Even if you're not a good writer, you can still write OK if you know your topic. Read first, then the writing is an exercise at the end of your course when you know the information well enough.

leahm74

HOW TO RAISE MONEY FOR SCHOOL FUNDS

We had some teachers who had a sense of humor. One time three of the male teachers agreed to have their legs waxed in front of an audience! It was great fun and we raised loads of money selling tickets to watch.

lili2008

Seniors

or What? I wish everyone would stop mumbling.

There are those who are defined as an age and those who are not. It's the Frisky versus the Owlish. Age is not a number anymore; it's an adjective. So when does "old" actually begin? While life expectancy has undoubtedly increased, the biggest change is that childbearing has ceased to be a predictable event, occurring anywhere from twenty-five to forty-five—if at all. Our perception of life stages has shifted drastically, and there is a view that anything can happen at any age. As a consequence, the sense of a slow slide into senility is gone. And "middle age" seems to have been abolished altogether—now we just stay young until we're old. Or maybe I'm just saying that because I'm forty.

HOW TO IMPROVE YOUR MARRIAGE AND NOT IRRITATE YOUR FRIENDS, CHILDREN, AND GRANDCHILDREN

To get out of the habit of bickering with your partner in public, make a point of drawing attention to it in private. Say, "I can only say this because we're alone," and then let fly. If you do it with good humor, it actually becomes a source of amusement.

Lala

HOW TO AGE HAPPILY

Taking care of yourself physically is important to aging happily; exercise, get regular checkups (don't forget the dentist), and practice moderation in dieting and sun exposure. But the most important thing is not to neglect your spiritual side. Prayer, mediation, and acts of kindness to others help you enjoy life and the wisdom of your years (especially if you volunteer at a nursing home or senior center).

Also, make sure you stay on top of your finances.

Masi

Never act your age. Act your shoe size.

At fifty-two I am still climbing trees, playing soccer in the park, gathering seashells, building sand castles, and trespassing into fields to steal apples! And exercise!

ladydigger

Flirt a little when you're talking to people; it always raises a smile.

LucyD

HOW TO KEEP YOUR MIND SHARP AS YOU AGE

Take a college correspondence course. It does wonders for morale, the mind, and the memory (with magnesium of course) and gives you something to look forward to. I got my first degree at fifty-six and two more since. It is my all-time favorite pastime.

Canopus

HOW TO BE GRACEFUL IN OLD AGE

Really concentrate on your posture—the older we get, the more inclined we are to be lazy and stoop. Above all, don't grunt and groan when you sit down and get up from a chair.

Lala

HOW TO FLATTER YOUR SKIN AS YOU AGE

Use a light-reflecting foundation, soft colors on the lips, and light-colored eye shadow—lilac is good. Also, if you have your hair colored, make the front just a little lighter than the rest; this really brightens up the face.

blondie5

Concentrate at least three times a day on cultivating a pleasant, welcoming, cheerful expression.

Troops

HOW TO IMPROVE YOUR APPEARANCE

Try, but not too hard. Remember, after forty there's a fine line between sexy and slut, so no bare midriffs off the beach, tattoos, or Goth eye makeup. If in doubt, ask your son or any other handy youth!

corkychum

HOW TO IMPROVE YOUR FIGURE AFTER SIXTY-FIVE

Buy a new bra and have it fitted properly.
We change. Accept it.

Gam

HOW TO ZIP UP THE BACK OF A DRESS OR TOP IF THERE'S NO ONE AROUND TO HELP YOU

Thread cotton or a long shoelace through the zip and pull up.

jennywd

HOW TO FIND A GOOD DATING WEBSITE IF YOU ARE SIXTY

Do you have any other single friends (male or female) of your age? If so, you could make a pact to try out a few dating agencies and websites together. To find the best sites, just spend a few hours online and see which appeal to you. All sites will ask you your age and interests and help you hook up with similar people. No matter what your age, the only real answer is just to get out there and do it! The more activities you sign up for, the more people you will meet, and the more likely you are to meet someone you like. Just be very cautious at the beginning with anyone you meet (either virtually or in reality); don't trust anyone until he has earned your trust!

Michelle

HOW TO FIND A SUITABLE MATE LATER IN LIFE

Volunteer for a cause you feel strongly about. This will increase your chances of finding someone with values similar to yours.

Jillaroo95

HOW TO BE EVERLASTINGLY PATIENT WITH A
DEAF COMPANION

It is often said that deafness is the loneliest disability. I think this is particularly true if the deafness occurs through injury or aging, and the deaf person has to struggle to learn lip reading and sign language as an adult. My grandmother—who was one of the smartest people I knew, really quick-witted—went very deaf, and she really got annoyed when people started to treat her as if she were stupid. Try to remember this when you communicate with your deaf friend.

MenopausalMadam

Several members of my family are somewhat deaf, and I find my best conversations take place on the telephone—when they hold the earpiece close to their heads, they hear much better. This has really helped to build relationships, as conversation is not so easy during big, noisy family parties.

Josa2

Having been temporarily profoundly deaf due to an ear infection, my top tips would be these:

Always position yourself in full facial view of the person you are speaking to so he/she can read your expression and lips; this way he can take a stab at what you are saying. Turning away even for a second can blow your chances of communication!

Don't shout from another room or away from the person;

he may hear your voice but not what you're saying, which is frustrating.

If you are approaching a deaf person, make some other noise like banging on the floor so he's aware you are there.

hilarygnorman

HOW TO GET OVER GROWING OLD ALONE

I'm old and I'm alone. I love it! I do what I want, when I want, have a great circle of friends, keep myself active, and by doing so, remain interesting.

Don't concentrate on yourself; look outward. If you hate your own company, everyone else will too.

Beachy1

Instead of thinking about the years ahead being alone, start thinking about all the things you want to do on your own before the new partner comes along.

My dad has found love again recently at his local senior citizens' Evergreen club, and he's eighty-three. He's no big Romeo but is just himself and does not pretend to be something he's not. If love can happen to him, it can happen to you, too.

Keep smiling at the world and saying yes to new opportunities—you never know what's just around the corner.

Mangogirl

HOW TO KEEP TRACK OF THINGS

For things like keys and wallets, put a box or basket on the hall table (or similar central spot) and put everything in it when you get home. I also have a dish for my earrings and watch, as I kept taking them off and leaving them all over the place. Things get lost when they don't really have a home, so give them one and then you'll use it.

distractedhousewife

HOW TO STAY YOUNG IN RETIREMENT

I am not retired; I am on permanent holiday. I wake up each morning and plan what to do that day. Life is wonderful.

Redlady

HOW TO AVOID FALLS

Always sit on the edge of the bed to put on or remove your underwear, tights, socks, pants, whatever. Older people regularly fall over when getting dressed or undressed.

Cali

Never, ever have uncarpeted stairs in your house. Chose something that has substance and isn't slippery.

Gam

HOW TO AVOID SLIPPING IN THE BATH

Lay your damp facecloth on the edge of the bath to give you a better grip when you get out.

Troops

HOW TO WARD OFF DOWAGER'S HUMP

To keep your shoulder muscles supple and strong and ward off dowager's hump, do the following Pilates exercise: Press your elbows into your waist and hold your hands out in front of you as though holding a tray. Then swivel your hands outward, keeping your elbows tight at your waist. Do six or seven back and forth whenever you think of it—at least four times a day.

Cali

HOW TO GET A JOB WHEN YOU'RE OVER SIXTY

Take your date of birth off your resume. That at least might get you an interview, and from there you can impress on merit. It has worked for people I know.

paulamessum

Style

or Maybe I'd better wear jeans after all.

Fashion is a funny old thing: Women you would consider to be accomplished, together, and the very definition of ball-busting are often scared witless of it. Teenagers who are too sheepish to look you in the eye just get it with a blithe insouciance that is stunning. And even though so much of fashion is about sex, it's got very little to do with the opposite sex. Add to all this the fact that you can nail the look one season but if you stop paying attention, trends can slip by, and suddenly you're back to square one on the feeling-like-a-badly-dressed-dork-o-meter. Fashion is surely one of the more complex issues we face. Luckily, we have the choice about when and at which level we wish to engage: clean and confident is all that really matters.

HOW TO STORE SMALL EARRINGS

Buy a pill sorter box and keep small earrings in it; the sections are just the right size.

Redlady

HOW TO ALWAYS LOOK PUT TOGETHER

Take a few minutes on Sunday evening with your calendar and decide what your week will be—X amount of work outfits, Y amount of social outfits. Make up the combinations you like on separate hangers, together with underwear and accessories. The first time you do this may take a little longer, but you will get it down to ten minutes max. This helps you to use all of your wardrobe, in different and sometimes unthought-of combinations. Notice what you don't wear and get creative with what you have. Saves money, too.

ashling

HOW TO GET NEW CLOTHES FROM OLD CLOTHES

Find a tailor or seamstress you feel you can trust—someone who measures carefully and pins gently! Bring in clothes you love but which need some sprucing up. The seamstress will be able to recommend what can be done to give the garment new life—perhaps nipping in the waist, subtly changing the collar, shortening the sleeves, or whatever. I did this some years ago with about twenty items of clothing. For under $200, I had what felt like twenty new items of clothing. Definitely worth the price to extend the life of your existing clothes without getting completely bored with them.

CeeVee

HOW TO GET RID OF STATIC ON CLOTHES

Rub a dryer sheet over the clothes. Even a used one will work.

stelladore

HOW TO MAKE YOURSELF MORE NOTICEABLE

It's simple—if you want to get noticed, wear red! I pulled off this trick the other day: I went to a meeting where I really wanted to be interviewed by the press about an issue that is very important to me, so I wore my red coat. Who was the first person the press came to? That's right, the woman in the red coat!

bekki007

HOW TO RIP/DISTRESS A PAIR OF OLD JEANS

Use sandpaper. You can use it to distress the denim gradually until you get the effect you want.

uber

When distressing jeans, put them in the wash after customizing as it will help to create that soft, frayed edge.

jones22

HOW TO SECURE BUTTONS

Don't lose any more buttons—just cover the top of the button with a layer of clear polish. Those loose bits of cotton will stay secure, and you won't be tempted to pick at them!

This is not suitable for buttons that are sewn on underneath, where you can't see any stitching.

elizabethcoteman

HOW TO WEAR A BACKLESS HALTER DRESS WHEN YOU'RE TOO FLAT-CHESTED BUT CAN'T WEAR A PADDED BRA

Get cups to sew into the dress! You can probably get them at a fabric store. That's what my tailor did for my wedding dress, and it was really comfortable.

kenosko

HOW TO REALLY CLEAR OUT YOUR CLOSET

Make an appointment for a charity to pick up unneeded clothes twice a year when you switch to your summer and winter clothes. It's a great way to get a fresh start, declutter, and take a tax deduction—all in one!

ckhokie02

HOW TO DECIDE WHICH SHOES TO KEEP WHEN DOWNSIZING YOUR SHOE COLLECTION

For the next month, each time you wear a pair of shoes put them away the wrong way around. At the end of the month you will see exactly which shoes you really wear. The rest will require a judgment call.

Maude

HOW TO REMEMBER GREAT OUTFITS

Whenever you wear an outfit you particularly like or get complimented on, take a picture of it and stick the picture on the inside of your closet door.

chocolatenoor

HOW TO BE ORGANIZED IF YOU USE SEVERAL HANDBAGS

Buy yourself some see-through zippered mesh bags or small makeup bags, then put all your personal maintenance stuff into one and all the "traveling office" things into the other. Not only will this make your handbag a lot tidier, but you can move the bags quickly from one handbag to another and get more use out of your handbag collection.

lizziecraig

HOW TO AVOID FASHION EMERGENCIES

If you have a few handbags you use all the time, fill a pocket in each with emergency supplies—safety pins, bandages, pain killer, lip balm, hair bands, etc.

LauraBailey

HOW TO STORE HANDBAGS SO YOU CAN SEE AND ACCESS THEM EASILY IN A SMALL SPACE

I've put a small rail with S hooks (think kitchen storage at Ikea!) on the back of my bedroom door. This is perfect for small evening-type bags. For larger bags, you can get larger rails that can be installed along a wall.

Toomanyshoes

HOW TO STRAIGHTEN THE BRIM OF A STRAW HAT

Hold it (carefully) over the hot steam from a boiling kettle and mold it back into shape.

Ali161

If it's supposed to be flat (like a boater-type hat), place it on a flat surface, weigh the brim down with heavy books, and leave it somewhere warm for a few days. That should straighten it out.

seagull-pie

HOW TO BE ORGANIZED FOR QUICK REPAIRS

Keep three or four needles threaded in different colors to match your clothes in a sewing kit. Keep the kit in your closet. That way when you take off your clothes and notice a button loose or hem unraveling, you can fix it quickly. You're more likely to do on-the-spot repairs and fix your clothes if you have needle and thread at hand.

ashling

HOW TO FIX A HEM IN AN EMERGENCY

Adhesive tape from a first-aid kit works really well—it's flexible, so you don't get a weird rigid line.

distractedhousewife

HOW TO FIX A LOOSE THREAD ON A SWEATER

A fine crochet hook is better than a needle for pulling tugged threads through to the back of knitwear. Just slide it through the knit, hook the errant thread, and pull it back—no need to fiddle with threading a needle. I keep a tiny crochet hook in my handbag for just this type of emergency; it's surprising how useful they are.

distractedhousewife

HOW TO GET RID OF PILLS FROM WOOL AND CASHMERE

Shave them off with a dry disposable razor.

ashleap

HOW TO GET SPILLED COCKTAILS OUT OF A RABBIT FUR COAT THAT HAS GOTTEN STICKY

It sounds like you have a fun life . . .

Unless you want to take it to a specialist cleaner, I would do what a rabbit would do and wash it off gently using plain water. Although you might want to use a dampened sponge instead of your tongue.

Tooke

HOW TO STOP A SNAG IN YOUR PANTYHOSE

If it's already slightly snagged, use transparent tape on the inside of the hose to stop the hole from getting bigger.

xsammyx

Wet a bar of soap very slightly and then rub around the run. When the soap dries it will act like starch and stiffen, thus stopping the hole from spreading. I have used this on many occasions and it never fails.

ladydigger

HOW TO REMOVE ODORS FROM VINTAGE CLOTHES WHEN DRY CLEANING DOESN'T WORK

Try rubbing dry baking soda into the affected areas. Leave for about two hours, then brush off thoroughly. Repeat the process if the smell lingers. It worked on my coat.

ladydigger

HOW TO KEEP SOCKS, STOCKINGS, ETC. TIDY

I put each pair of pantyhose in its own little clear bag (such as a food bag) and label it with a description—e.g., black opaque, diamond, fishnet. This helps identify them quickly as they all look the same when they are in a mess in my drawer.

princess87

HOW TO CLEAN LIGHT-COLORED SUEDE OR
NUBUCK SHOES

Take the soft bit from the center of a piece of bread, squash it, then lightly rub it over any stains to lift them.

mimi18

HOW TO GET WATER STAINS OFF LEATHER BOOTS

First, clean the area with saddle soap, rinse using a damp soft cloth, and dry. Then lightly apply mink oil and rub into all areas affected—this softens the leather and helps seal against more staining, making the next cleaning easier. If you desire, get a can of sealer/protectant and spray all outer areas of the boots. (The mink oil and/or sealer spray may darken the color somewhat.)

333robin

HOW TO GIVE SHOE SOLES BETTER GRIP

Stick those nonslip tub decals on the bottom of your shoes.

cstar_1

HOW TO STOP A SHOE FROM SQUEAKING

Try putting talcum powder in the shoes. It makes your feet
smell nice, too.

blondie5

HOW TO STOP SHOES FROM SLIPPING OFF YOUR FEET

If your shoes slip off your feet at the back as you walk or
dance, spray the area with firm-hold hairspray just before you
put them on.

distractedhousewife

HOW TO STRETCH SHOES

If your shoes are made of a natural fabric, pack them tightly
with wet newspaper. As the newspaper dries the paper expands, stretching the shoe slightly.

If your shoes are manmade, the fabric may split if you attempt to stretch them too much.

dingdongthewitch

Technology

or Catch me if you can.

To talk about "technology" as a separate entity is terribly old-fashioned. Young people don't talk about it in that way; to them it's just part of life. Like breathing. If you're over thirty-five beware of this—it's a dead giveaway, especially if you're dating a younger person. Technology is also the ultimate frenemy, because while it appears that that sparkly new, supercool gadget will add zing to everything from your work life to your sex life it will also make you utterly dependent on others (to fix it when it goes wrong), to a degree you haven't experienced since you were lying in an incubator. To this extent the claim that technology is "empowering" is only partly true.

HOW TO EXTEND THE LIFE OF A PHONE BATTERY

If you really want to increase your time between charges, try deselecting things you don't need. Bluetooth uses a lot of power, as does Wi-Fi, so if you're not using those, switch 'em off. GPS? Kills your battery, so don't use it if you don't need to. The flash for the camera? Takes a fair bit of power, so don't take photos in the dark.

myfavoritesock

HOW TO CONSERVE POWER WHEN YOUR COMPUTER BATTERY IS RUNNING LOW

If you're working on a computer with a rapidly fading battery (and you don't need the Internet), turn off your wireless access; it really chews up battery power.

Tooke

Reduce the brightness to about 40 percent when listening to music, avoid fully discharging the battery, remember to put it on sleep mode when you're not using it, and most important, keep it cool and out of the hot sun.

Ruth

HOW TO KEEP YOUR COMPUTER SAFE

Make sure you have antivirus, antispyware programs and a firewall. Keeping them all up to date will significantly reduce the number of problems you'll get. There are good free programs for all of these, just use common sense, and remember, prevention is better than a cure.

Nova7

HOW TO UNDERSTAND YOUR GEEK

1. Remember, size *is* everything. If they buy a 50-inch LCD screen, it's because they think things genuinely look better the bigger they seem. Don't complain, just sit further back on the sofa.
2. If they buy one album by a band and like it, it is imperative that they then get every other album by that band. Absolutely imperative.
3. Occasional sex would be quite nice but is less important than an enormous TV.

   myfavoritesock

HOW TO KNOW IF A WEBSITE IS SECURE

It's always a worry when you enter credit card details online, but there are ways to minimize the risk. First, on pages where you enter financial details, the first characters of the URL (long text string at the top) should change from "http://" to "https://" (secure mode). In addition, a padlock icon should appear in the bottom of the browser window. If you're still unsure, check to see if the company has a reasonable customer care setup (call and ask them what they do with credit card details following a purchase) or do a Google search on "companyname + complaints." If other people have had big problems—don't use the site!

myfavoritesock

HOW TO PROMOTE YOUR BLOG

In most forums there is a signature box under your post where you can enter the link to your blog. Make it look nice—bold it, center it.

Also, on Facebook or Myspace there is always a space for your web address.

priscillaaa

HOW TO SPEED UP YOUR COMPUTER

Start >
Control Panel >
Internet Options >
Delete Temporary Files (including cookies/pop-up ads/
  etc.—picture shows a cabinet being emptied of paper)

If there is lots of info, it will take a long time. Click OK
when finished.

toptiptwin

HOW TO FIX STICKY KEYS ON A RECENTLY TEA-SOAKED KEYBOARD

Make sure your keyboard is unplugged/switched off, grab an
old toothbrush, wrap a baby wipe around the bristles, and
gently rub. You can do the same thing using a swizzle stick to
get into the awkward places.

funnygirlshell

HOW TO REMEMBER PASSWORDS

There are a lot of services that require you to change your
password periodically, and sometimes you are not allowed to
use your previous ten passwords. It is a safety measure but can

be annoying. You can cheat the system by just using the same word and increasing the number—password1, password2, and so on; then come back to password1. You could use the current month as the number as well; whatever works for your memory. But never write it down.

navstips

Why not change it to something that is on your desk? That way when you forget your password, you can just look around your work space and think, "Ah yes, my password was *pen!*"

PollyPops

I work in a call center and most people use their kids' names, but my favorite password was . . . *iveforgotten!* Genius.

jayneym

HOW TO MAKE SURE YOUR CHILDREN ARE SAFE ONLINE

The bottom line is that, as long as you know less about your computer and the Internet than your eight-year-old does, you can't control or monitor what he/she does online. Ultimately, if you want to keep them safe, come to grips with the technology. The best way to know what your kids are doing is to be there when they use the computer and then be very honest and upfront with them should they stumble upon something untoward (and they will). As they get older, you will have less and less control over what they can and cannot look at (remember, theirs is the first generation to have always had Internet access from their mobile phones), so the best thing you can do is equip them now to deal with the unsavory stuff on the Internet in an open and honest way!

    davlinds

Keep their computer in a public place such as the family room or kitchen with the screen facing the room.

    Tooke

Travel

or When can we go home?

When traveling most of the things that make life irritating are compounded by the fact that one has always forgotten something crucial, particularly at the rental car office. Rental car offices are God's way of telling us that he meant it about the trial and tribulation stuff. Even the prelude to a holiday can be infinitely stressful—expectations are so high and you have so much to do before you go that the statistical chances of your being relaxed on vacation are very, very low. Unless you are sedated. For couples, all the handy distractions, whether they be friends, sports, cinema, or shopping, that prevent bickering from turning into domestic homicide are removed at a stroke. And replaced by a 24/7 argument about who drives, where the nearest grocery store is, why he didn't buy "basics," and why you forgot to order a baby seat for the rental. And yet . . . all those blissfully happy framed photographs hanging in your home are the result of surviving all of the above and enjoying the good parts.

HOW TO BARTER/HAGGLE

I did this in Turkey every time I bought something and it worked every time!

Ask the price of something without your boyfriend or male friend or husband around. (If you're on your own this works, too.) See what price they give you, then say politely, "I think I will have to check with my husband." Go around a corner out of sight and take bills out of your purse in the amount you are actually willing to pay, head back, and tell them your husband would only give you X amount to spend.

Every time I did this the salesman respected the decision of "the husband" and would take the amount I offered. Easy negotiating, with no hassle whatsoever!

nellyprdirector

HOW TO AVOID UNWANTED ADVANCES FROM MEN WHILE TRAVELING

Move with purpose and as if you know where you're going, even if you don't. Men will often approach women who look unsure, since this can be perceived as a sign of weakness, and predatory types tend to take advantage of that. They are less apt to approach a confident-looking woman. However, some men like a challenge, so if they still approach you, I suggest giving them a blank, unwavering stare until they go away.

Jillaroo95

HOW TO BUILD THE PERFECT SAND CASTLE WITH YOUR CHILDREN

Damp sand (not wet) makes the best sand castles. Have the children direct how it will be made and put yourself in the position of their "helper." Bring shells and stones and have them decorate the castle. Ask them to tell you the story behind this particular castle.

Jillaroo95

HOW TO DO SOMETHING USEFUL WHEN YOU'RE TRAVELING

Before you go, check out www.StuffYourRucksack.com to see if you can take something that's needed wherever you're going. It might be pencils for a school or a football for an orphanage— places and requests are listed. This is a brilliant idea that really deserves support.

Cali

Check out the local culture and see if you would like to learn something from them. Cooking courses are popular where you learn the local cuisine (especially in Thailand). Learning a new skill is always very fulfilling.

If you are traveling to a third world country, do some research into programs that help the less fortunate and see what they are asking for.

Beulah

HOW TO DRESS COMFORTABLY ON SAFARI

When traveling in Africa wear a support bra for the safari. *Very* bumpy roads. *Great* adventure!

Sheila

HOW TO FIND GREAT LOCAL RESTAURANTS
WHEN TRAVELING

Often when you ask your hotel's concierge or doorman for restaurant suggestions, you'll get the name of whichever restaurant has given the biggest bribe. So try asking the porter or someone lower down the "food chain" in the hotel's staff. They are less likely to have been paid off.

Monica

HOW TO TRAVEL WITH A BABY AND ARRIVE
LOOKING UNSCATHED

Accept that you are going to end up wearing whatever you've fed your child and that you won't be able to change—so wear black and carry a fresh bright scarf to wear on arrival.

happycanadian

HOW TO SURVIVE LONG FLIGHTS WITH SMALL CHILDREN

Having traveled ten-hour flights with children every year since they were born, I've learned to go to a novelty store a week or so before the flight and buy small, inexpensive games or toys—they occupy children only for a short while, and it doesn't matter if they get lost. Here is the trick: Wrap them individually and mark them 1, 2, 3, 4, etc.—one set for each child. Let them see them and tell them that they won't open #1 until they are at the boarding gate, #2 after the meal is cleared away. For my kids it was a perfect distraction and reward—right up to the last one on arrival. (Don't forget to leave one end of each package open so that it can be inspected if necessary.)

happycanadian

HOW TO DRIVE ON THE CORRECT SIDE OF THE ROAD IN A FOREIGN COUNTRY

Get a bright colored sticker with an arrow on it pointing in the direction of correct lane. Stick it on the steering wheel. This way you see it as soon as you get in the car, and keep on checking.

pandsy

HOW TO DRIVE SAFELY IN SNOW AND ICE

Keep an old piece of carpet at least 1 foot x 3 feet in your car to put under a spinning tire—more effective than salt or grit, which can just disappear into the snow.

Culi

Being in a higher gear does help, and you can even do it in most automatic cars. Check whether there's a gear lock button to lock you into second or third.

Troops

HOW TO KNOW WHICH SIDE YOUR GAS TANK IS ON WHEN PULLING UP AT THE PUMP WITH A RENTAL CAR

If you look at the fuel gauge (on the dashboard) you'll see a little gas pump icon; the handle (there may also be an arrow) on the pump indicates which side of your car the filler tank is on. So, if the handle on the pump is on the right or the arrow points to the right, your tank will be on the right side of your car. If it's on the left, then it's on the left side.

JulieG

HOW TO FRESHEN THE WAY YOUR CAR SMELLS

A few drops of your favorite essential oil on a dampened cotton ball is a good idea. You will have to refresh it every few days, but it's a pleasant and natural way to freshen your car.

ashling

Buy bar soap in a scent that pleases you and just leave it in a paper bag in the car. It emits a clean, light smell.

DezG

HOW TO KEEP THE KIDS QUIET IN THE CAR

If the kids are fighting and refuse to be quiet, turn on Bach's Toccata and Fugue in B minor at full volume. It renders them speechless and teaches them something at the same time.

cougar

HOW TO STOP YOUR EARS FROM HURTING DURING AIRPLANE LANDINGS

When learning to scuba dive you have to equalize your ears as you dive deeper—the same technique works in airplanes and high-rise elevators! In scuba you're taught to (1) take a deep breath, (2) close your mouth and squeeze your nose shut, and (3) slowly, gently try to exhale—since your mouth and nose are shut, it forces the air to your ears and works to equalize them.

DezG

HOW TO PACK CARRY-ON TOILETRIES

When the salesperson is packing up your cosmetic purchases, ask if there are any samples "because I have an upcoming trip." Since you've just made a purchase, they are much more likely to share samples (and more of them) than they'd be for random sample-moochers. Plus, since these are products you're already using, you can be assured that your travel kit won't result in adverse reactions! Make sure all your samples fit in a single quart-size, zip-top, clear plastic bag and pack it in your carry-on. Don't wait until just before landing to start freshening up—everyone else will be doing the same thing, and you can't relax while people are banging on the restroom door!

DezG

HOW TO AVOID TUMMY UPSETS WHEN TRAVELING

Wherever you are traveling try to eat the local yogurt. This has local bacteria and may help you avoid an upset stomach.

    rosepink

HOW TO STOP TRAVEL SICKNESS

Put your middle and index fingers on your wrist (as if you were taking your pulse) and apply pressure; this should ease the sick feeling.

    Flourescent Adolescent

HOW TO GET CHEAPER RAIL FARES

In many cases, if you are traveling with two or more friends, you can get a group discount if you buy all the tickets together rather than individually. Then just split the lower total cost. A very friendly ticket attendant once gave me and my friends this tip.

    ohknickers

HOW TO PACK A STRAW HAT IN YOUR CHECKED LUGGAGE SO THAT IT DOESN'T COME OUT A CRUSHED MESS AT THE OTHER END

Stuff the hat with socks or underwear and then carefully pack other clothes around it. That way it doesn't get squashed. Obviously don't pack it right next to or under heavy things like shoes or books.

Anita123

HOW TO PACK SHOES

The little plastic shower caps that you get in hotels are great for packing shoes—they keep the rest of your clothes as well as your shoes separate and protected. Also, place socks, underwear, etc. inside your shoes.

Deborah

HOW TO PREVENT BOTTLES FROM LEAKING WHILE TRAVELING

Before you pack your plastic bottles for a plane trip, gently squeeze some of the air out of the bottle and then close tightly—no more leaking bottles when you arrive at your destination.

bobbie

HOW TO TRAVEL LONG TERM WITH ABSOLUTE
MINIMAL CLOTHING

When backpacking for a year I learned to take only black underwear, so it could double as a bathing suit wherever I ended up swimming. In Egypt, black panties and a black tee shirt worked in the Nile.

happycanadian

HOW TO DEAL WITH LOSS OF MONEY, PASSPORT, ETC.

Before you travel send yourself an email that contains the following:

a scan of your passport, your credit card issuers' contact telephone numbers, serial numbers of traveler's checks, airline ticket numbers and contact details for the airline, contact details for next of kin, and any other similar information that may be lost while traveling. If you have a problem you can usually access your email and get the info you need to put things right.

rosepink

Weddings

or It's not about the big day, it's about the days after.

It is little wonder that many women go insane on their wedding day. For some, it is the culmination of every game of Barbie they ever played, every episode of *American Idol* they ever watched, and every date they ever went on. A girl's wedding day is so hyped up as the Best Day of Your Life that the accompanying hysteria is no surprise. Women seem to have comprehensively hijacked the day, such that the groom is no more than a prop. Unmarried at the time of writing, I make no promise that one day I will not also fall into this seductive trap. However, I suspect that it isn't any individual's day, it's the couple's day, and the way to get through it is to form a strong alliance with your other half and politely tell everyone else to back off. If the two of you can put on a half-decent wedding in the presence of two or more fractious tribes, then raising a tribe of your own from birth to leaving college should be a piece of cake.

HOW TO KEEP YOUR MOTHER UNDER CONTROL WHEN PLANNING YOUR WEDDING

First of all, you have to remember that she has probably been thinking about this day (on and off) since the day you were born. OK, so it's *your* day and all, but have a little compassion for the woman who looked after you all those years. (It'll also be kinda weird for her to see her baby all grown up and married, and she may be facing some "I'm-getting-old" issues of her own.) So try to include her as much as you can, and maybe even give her certain jobs of her own (not just the boring ones) so she can really feel she's had some input. She's probably not trying to take over, but just wants to feel included.

Regina

HOW TO SET A WEDDING DATE

Before you name the date, check for any potential sporting events (like the Super Bowl) or other major events that may conflict with dates you are considering.

Flavia

HOW TO GET A GOOD PRICE ON YOUR ENGAGEMENT RING

Do your research! Spend a little time on the web researching and comparing prices—bluenile.com is a good place to start. That way you can see how much you should be paying for a certain size and type of stone. Then, when you go to the jewelry store, you'll be in a much stronger position to bargain. Also, if you avoid the big jewelry chains and look for independents and boutiques, you are far more likely to get a discount (up to 30 percent), as they know that people tend to return to the place they bought their engagement rings.

Brittany

HOW TO HAVE A GREAT WEDDING DAY

Plan it so that on the actual day of your wedding you have nothing to do apart from getting ready, and no one is expecting you to write place cards or do anything else. You should give yourself that one day.

Rowena

HOW TO RELAX ABOUT YOUR BOYFRIEND'S PENDING BACHELOR PARTY

Just make sure you have a fabulous bachelorette party and don't worry about what he is getting up to. Being obsessed and questioning him is a sure turnoff and will make him not want to talk to you about stuff. Enjoy your night out and let him enjoy his!

DOZIGGY

HOW TO PLAN A HOT-WEATHER WEDDING (ESPECIALLY FOR BRIDES WHO GET SWEATY WHEN NERVOUS!)

On my wedding day with my hair up, makeup done, and all ready to rock and roll down the aisle, I stripped down and sat in an ice cold bath for twenty minutes before getting dressed. I had heard that marathon runners do this after training as it cools their bodies right down and lasts for ages. It worked very well, and I got through a whole hour in a packed church during the scariest moment of my life without breaking as much as one bead of sweat. That made my wedding day. I had been so scared about how unattractive a sweaty bride would look. This is the answer: It may not be comfortable but it works, and since then for any potentially hot and uncomfortable occasion where looking good and cool is key . . . on goes the cold bath!

Amber

HOW A BRIDESMAID CAN REALLY HELP OUT BEFORE THE BIG DAY

Offer to run errands for the bride or even be her chauffeur for the day. There are always so many little things to be done and using public transportation makes them twice as hard.

Noreen

HOW TO BE AWARE OF THE MOST IMPORTANT BRIDESMAID DUTY

Helping your friend go to the bathroom if she's wearing an enormous dress is it! Someone else can do pretty much everything else, but if the dress is bigger than the toilet stall she's going to need some pretty intimate help.

Kaitlyn

HOW TO THANK YOUR YOUNGER BRIDESMAIDS ON YOUR WEDDING DAY

Make up some of your own goodie bags. They'll be less expensive and more personal than buying something ready-made. Fill little fabric bags with toys, sweets, and games for them to play with during the day. With a larger budget, add in one larger gift they can keep as a present for being your bridesmaid.

Larissa

HOW TO HAVE ECO-FRIENDLY, CHEAP CONFETTI

Remove rose petals before the flowers open and store in a container in the freezer. On the day of the wedding take them out and either leave natural or spray with a scent.

Marina

HOW TO NEGOTIATE A FAIR PRICE FOR CORKAGE

Do this before you book the venue. If you make it clear that the reservation depends on how negotiable they are, you might be able to get a good deal. Do speak to someone who is higher up; this person must have the authority to make a decision. Be willing to compromise, too. If they're not willing to reduce corkage, find out what else they can do.

rooi_skoene

HOW TO SAVE MONEY ON YOUR WEDDING

Ask your local horticultural college if it has students who could do your flowers or ask a staff member at a local florist if he or she does private work (be discreet about this though). Have only two courses for your meal. Look for your dress in the sales. Ask your local culinary school if anyone can make your cake, or buy an iced fruit or sponge cake and decorate it yourself.

COLIYTYHE

Go on eBay for napkins, place cards, etc. to match your chosen color scheme. It's usually much cheaper than having printed cards done. If you know someone who has lovely handwriting, ask them to write out the place cards. You can print your own invitations using clip art and some nice colored card stock. Venues are often cheaper midweek than on weekends.

COLIYTYHE

People tend to overspend on flowers. In a church, you really need only two arrangements, on either side of the altar. That is where people will be looking, and most churches are beautiful enough without flowers all up the aisles. Also, look into whether anyone else is getting married on the same day in your church, so you can share the cost. Make the arrangements dramatic by having lots of foliage, but with enough large white flowers for contrast.

Joan

Definitely get friends to drive you to and from your wedding and reception. I was driven to the church by one of my parents' best friends (lovely for him and me) and went away in my husband's beat-up old car (an old jalopy covered in foam and tin cans), driven by a nondrinking friend wearing a borrowed chauffeur's cap. It was more meaningful for all of us, the guests got it, and it cost nothing.

Esme

There is absolutely no shame in asking for donations toward your honeymoon instead of a present, and your honeymoon doesn't have to be expensive. A long weekend somewhere nice (and then returning home quietly and taking the phone off the hook for a week!) will be just as romantic and memorable as a two-week safari and believe me, all you will want to do is sleep anyway, so don't plan anything too busy.

AbChis

HOW TO PLAN A GREAT HONEYMOON WHEN YOU'RE ON A BUDGET

Look closer to home. Stop and ask yourself what you want from a honeymoon. Is it adventure and exploration or just a week in bed with new hubby and wine? If the latter, renting a cottage in another part of the country can be cheaper with much less hassle. Who says a big bed and a log fire isn't as romantic as sun, sea, and sand?

gduffy85

We registered on travelersjoy.com and our guests gave us money for the trip; we are planning to go to Thailand next year. We wanted to take a nice long trip but didn't want to suddenly rush off after the ceremony. So we spent a few nice days in Napa after the wedding, and next December we'll be in Thailand!

Heather

HOW TO ENSURE PERFECT WEDDING PHOTOS

I have been to a few weddings recently where one or two of those disposable cameras were on each table at the reception. While the professional photos were being taken, many guests amused themselves by taking candid shots of each other, the minister having a little drink, the kids up to no good, etc. The cameras were gathered up at the end of the evening by a groomsman and developed.

MenopausalMadam

HOW TO FIND A GREAT WEDDING PHOTOGRAPHER WITHOUT GETTING RIPPED OFF

Ask your local college if any of its final-year photography students do private work.

ahlh

HOW TO INCORPORATE THE "SOMETHING BORROWED" INTO YOUR WEDDING OUTFIT

Need to add a "something borrowed" into your wedding ensemble but don't want to spoil your look? How about grabbing a quick squirt of one of your mom's perfumes on your way out? That way you don't end up wearing that necklace/bracelet/ring that a well-meaning family member has foisted on you but that doesn't match your chosen "look." Simple.

fionab

HOW TO INCORPORATE THE "SOMETHING BLUE" INTO YOUR WEDDING OUTFIT

Traditionally, the bride wore a garter with a blue ribbon or had a blue ribbon stitched inside her dress. You can be much more inventive though, wearing a piece of jewelry with a blue stone, blue nail polish (best for the toes!), blue lingerie, blue makeup (eye shadow, glitter, eyeliner, or mascara), a little blue handbag to keep lipstick and tissues handy, or a blue-trimmed hankie— just in case! Alternatively, have some blue flowers or blue ribbon in your bouquet, or use some blue confetti.

Tegan

Work

or It's hard, but it can be fun.

It is easy to forget that work is meant to be difficult; that's why it's called work. But while the workplace is never likely to be as soothing as a spa, it can be enriching and fulfilling and fun. If you look closely enough, there is indeed a shaded area on the Venn diagram of *difficult* and *fun*. They say the most important decision you can make is the person you choose to marry, but I believe it's the people you choose to work with. With your partner, you may spend an hour together in the morning, perhaps four in the evening (of which two are often child-related), and the rest of your time together, you're asleep. Whereas you are likely to spend at least eight totally sentient hours a day with your colleagues. With this in mind, choose wisely.

HOW TO COPE WITH BITCHING AT WORK

Hear and see all, repeat nothing.

carolyno001

This is so easy and it works every time. Be nice to others. I mean so overwhelmingly nice that they have nowhere to go with their bitchiness without looking like total idiots. Be a disgustingly saccharine sweet little angel and you will really confuse them!

runsfar

HOW TO GET AHEAD AT WORK WHEN YOU'RE THE ONLY WOMAN IN THE OFFICE

Stop thinking of being female as a disadvantage, for a start. In this day and age office managers are rarely the sexist pigs they were in the seventies and if you show potential, they'll recognize and reward it. Just don't back away from a challenge. If you don't like chairing meetings or giving presentations, get yourself on a course to overcome your fears. Let your manager know that if he's looking for a second-in-command, you can be relied on. In my experience getting ahead comes down to putting in the hard work, not what gender you are.

LindaCee

HOW TO MAKE A STUPID MALE COLLEAGUE STOP STARING AT YOU ALL THE TIME

Just look him straight in the eye and ask, "Are you all right?" If he says, "Yes, why?" just say, "You were staring at me and I wondered if there was something wrong." That way you're putting the ball in his court and forcing him to excuse himself. The shiftier and more uncomfortable you are, the more encouraged he'll feel—you need to meet him head-on in a nonaggressive manner.

TizzysMum

HOW TO STOP YOUR BOSS (OR ANYONE) FROM MAKING PASSES AT YOU

Use unfriendly body language and "blade" him with your body (i.e., turn so you are side on to him—if it is a him!). Don't stand with an open stance; this will make you look approachable.

DOZIGGY

HOW TO GET A COWORKER TO STOP TRYING TO PICK YOU UP

Have someone take a "snuggly" picture of yourself and a hot male friend. Send yourself flowers; you know you deserve them anyway. Then the next time your "buddy" comes around, excitedly show him a picture of your new beau and the flowers he sent you.

MargaretMM

HOW TO DEAL WITH A MARRIED BOSS WHO WANTS TO TAKE YOU OUT ON A DATE AND YOU DON'T WANT TO GO

I've been in this situation and you've got to be completely up front with him. Say, "You're married, and I don't do married men, so no thanks." Say it with a smile, and if you think his ego maybe needs a bit of a massage, prefix your comment with, "If you weren't married, things might possibly be different, but you are, so . . ."

These days bosses can't get away with threatening your career if you don't play their game, so just be polite but firm with him.

LindaCee

HOW TO PROOFREAD EFFECTIVELY AND ACCURATELY

First, print the material in hard copy. As you read through it, run your finger under each word slowly and say it aloud (feel free to close the door to your office/conference room/whatever). When you hear text spoken slowly, you catch some of the things that your brain otherwise reads into the draft when viewing on the computer screen.

DezG

HOW TO STAY CONSTANTLY MOTIVATED IN A CHALLENGING NEW JOB

I find it hard to be motivated unless I'm working toward a specific goal. Find a worthwhile goal (e.g., promotion, special project, bonus, window office, maintaining employment for at least a year in this terrible economy, having all the VPs know your name within six months, whatever), figure out the realistic steps to get there, and use that to motivate you. To the extent possible, add visual aids to your office/cubicle/etc., from a photo of the islands you'd visit if you got that bonus, to a picture of the local skyline you'd see from that window office, to a magazine photo of a lady in a fancy business suit—anything to help you refocus when you start drifting off.

DezG

HOW TO STOP BEING A WORKAHOLIC

There are two ways you can look at this: The first is to look at the underlying reasons why you are a workaholic. Is your self-worth tied to your work? Is your home life bad? Do you feel indispensable? Once you've narrowed down the why, then do something about it. Get counseling or do something about the home situation or realize that, realistically speaking, no one is truly indispensable. Or, if your workaholic tendency is a family trait that comes naturally to you, then the best way to deal with it is to wean yourself away from it in small steps, slowly, so that you can adjust. Perhaps start by not working so long on weekends. Then stop working altogether on weekends. Then go from there. That's what I did, and I'm happy to say I'm no longer a workaholic.

Jillaroo95

HOW TO STOP SLOUCHING OVER YOUR DESK AND CORRECT TERRIBLE POSTURE

My grandfather, who was an upholsterer, always said that the key to avoiding slouching in a chair is to make sure the chair is the right height for you. Your legs should bend at 90 degrees, and if you're slouching over a desk, it means your desk isn't high enough. Stick a telephone directory under each corner and see if that makes a difference.

bekki007

HOW TO FEEL LESS SELF-CONSCIOUS WHEN GIVING A PRESENTATION

Think of it as a mechanism to keep you on top of your game. People who are not self-conscious tend to be a bit too relaxed when they should be making their best effort, and it shows. By using your self-consciousness as a tool, it will become less of a burden to you and more of a plus.

Jillaroo95

HOW TO GET A PAY RAISE OR PROMOTION

Ask! Of course, first do your research. Know what is realistic in the marketplace and in your company. Be prepared with lists of your accomplishments, duties/tasks you perform that might be considered above your current position, accolades (from clients, peers, superiors), or volunteer work you do that benefits the company, etc. Be flexible; if they can't give you a raise, what about stock options, a bonus, or extra vacation? If they can't promote you, is there a lateral move that has more career advancement opportunities? If the answer is no, ask what you need to improve or accomplish to get where you want to go (management training? public speaking experience?). Do it and then ask again. Note that timing is everything, so don't ask at the end of a profit-losing quarter or as the company is filing for bankruptcy.

DezG

HOW TO LEARN LINES

These work for me:

1. For long speeches, use a plain postcard and work your way down, covering your next line.
2. For quick-fire dialogue, record the other person's lines onto an MP3 file (Audacity is a good program for this),

transfer them to your iPod, and work through the scene while traveling.

3. Once you know a scene quite well, trade favors with a neighbor to hear you.

4. For verse, dance.

5. For tough stuff with lots of metaphor and imagery, draw connected pictures in your head (or on your script). But most important:

6. However tired you are, always learn a scene the evening after rehearsing it.

Incidentally, if you find there's a particular bit you always forget, it might mean you haven't properly connected the character's thoughts behind the lines.

Lemming

HOW TO CALL IN SICK CONVINCINGLY

I think the worst thing you can do is get someone to call in on your behalf. Most of us, even at death's door, can manage a brief phone call, and I always get suspicious if a partner or friend contacts me. If you're going to take a sickie, keep the excuse simple and don't put on that fake "I'm so sick" voice. Don't forget what was the matter with you when you return to work in case anyone asks if you're feeling better.

zannathetrainer

HOW TO DEAL WITH A CLIENT WHO TREATS YOU LIKE A SERVANT, JUST EMAILING "ORDERS," AND IS DIFFICULT TO BUILD A RAPPORT WITH

This client may be a fast-paced, task-oriented person. That doesn't mean he's treating you like a servant; this is just the most efficient way of communicating. When it comes to business, not everyone feels the need to be chummy and tell you to have a nice day. Don't resent this person—instead, appreciate the fact that he's doing his best to not use up much of your time.

Jillaroo95

HOW TO DEAL WITH A COLLEAGUE WHO NETWORKS AT SOCIAL EVENTS IN A VERY "ME ME ME" WAY, CONSTANTLY LOOKING OVER THE SHOULDER OF ANYONE SHE IS TALKING TO

If it's your shoulder she is looking over, why not ask a direct question like, "Who exactly are you looking for?" It may be that this person is not fully aware she is doing it, and asking the question may focus her attention a bit more. If the behavior annoys you that much, excuse yourself from her company and go mingle with other people who annoy you less.

numptieheid

HOW TO SURVIVE IF YOU'RE SINGLE, HAVE BEEN UNEMPLOYED FOR NEARLY TWO YEARS, HAVE LIVED ON WELFARE FOR TOO LONG, AND HAVE RUN OUT OF SAVINGS

First thing is get out of the house. Go for a walk every day—I know this might sound ridiculous but it's amazing how this will clear your head and give you more energy. Get into a routine! Keep yourself healthy and stay focused on what you ultimately want. Also take a look at your belongings—anything you haven't used for two years, sell at a yard sale or on eBay— this will keep you going until you land a job.

mimi18

HOW TO MAKE YOUR RESUME STAND OUT

Have a look online for examples, but basically just keep to relevant information; don't go back through every job you had when you were sixteen. Keep the layout clear and precise and limit it to one page. Another good tip is to buy some heavy, good-quality cream paper and envelopes; a nice cream clean sheet, unfolded, will make a good presentation and stand out well amid a large pile of white sheets.

JemmaLittlefair

HOW TO DRESS FOR AN INTERVIEW

That really depends on the job! Try observing what people at your proposed new employment wear by visiting the work site when people are arriving for work or breaking for lunch. Use that as a guide, but bump it up a notch more formal for the interview. Avoid anything that is too sexy or too loud, or advertises too many brand logos. Don't wear flip-floppy mules or similar noisy shoes. Don't wear too much perfume or jewelry. Make sure everything fits well, both standing and sitting. If something needs to be altered (tighter or looser), get it done; otherwise you'll look sloppy.

DezG

HOW TO RELAX AT INTERVIEWS

Be as prepared as possible. Do your research on the company either on the net or by reading the annual report. Make sure you know your way to the interview and be there ten minutes early. Get a good night's sleep and have a decent breakfast. Get your outfit ready the night before, down to shoes and accessories. Make sure shoes are polished and whatever you wear is clean, with hems and buttons fixed. Don't exaggerate your resume. Practice the answers to odd questions like, Why should we hire you? and What are your weaknesses?—the type of question that might throw you for a loop. Last, practice deep breathing to calm yourself, and you will be fine.

ashling

What really helped me is having a friend interview me before I went to the actual meeting. But make sure the friend is serious about it and offers some feedback. My friend actually asked harder questions than my interviewers!

stelladore

HOW TO SURVIVE A TWO-MONTH INTERNSHIP IF YOU HATE IT

For my internship I was asked to type phone numbers into a database, which should have taken a month; but I got in early and stayed late (answering the phones when no one else was available—often for the boss, who thereby got to know my name), finished the job fast, then made myself useful to people who were working on things that looked more interesting. By the end of the month, I had secured my first job and stayed with the company for thirteen years.

Abi1973

HOW TO COPE WITH BEING LAID OFF

Take a weekend off to regroup (yes, just one weekend). Next, think big picture: This is about the global economy, not necessarily all about you or your performance. *But* it is a good opportunity to do some self-evaluation: Were you happy at the job? Are there additional credentials that would make you more marketable? Were there areas of weakness that you could improve? Then, figure out the next steps: Do you need another job(s) now? Can you afford (time and money) to get additional education/training? Do you want to switch careers? Make a game plan and schedule—resume, career counseling, headhunters, job searches, networking, etc.—and stick to it like it *is* your full-time job (i.e., eight hours a day, five days a week).

DezG

acknowledgments

WITH THANKS TO

Renee Joyce at Tangent, our online developer. She is the buffer between me and the tech team; her patience and good nature in the face of sometimes maddening technical issues are awe inspiring. (For those of you who don't work in the online world: Websites are never finished and bugs crop up for no apparent reason—it's like your fridge spontaneously unplugs itself to go sit in your bathroom every time your back is turned.)

Kate Lee and Karolina Sutton at ICM and Curtis Brown, respectively. They are wonderful women, without whom these books would have been a pipe dream.

Heather Lazare at Crown; she is a new and brilliant ally.

Intrusive Derek.

Enormous thanks to all the tipsters who visit TopTips.com and daily share their wisdom and advice. LindaCee, Jillaroo95, and DezG deserve special mentions—they are consistently brilliant, insightful, and funny.

My mother, who has always had a slightly irritating obsession with the use of language and grammar (inherited from her own mother, and I suspect is in the process of transferring it

to me by osmosis). Bored of fighting it, I harnessed that obsession and asked for her help in editing this book. Here is an
exchange of our emails when she had finished correcting the
spelling and grammar:

> From: Polly Wood
> To: Kate Reardon
> Sent: Thursday, July 23, 2009 7:35 PM
> Subject: finished
> DONE.
> OK, so what do I get?

> From: Kate Reardon
> To: Polly Wood
> Sent: Friday, July 24, 2009 10:34 AM
> Subject: Re: finished
>
> My eternal love and gratitude and the satisfaction
> of a job well done, as well as knowing that you are
> continuing to fulfill your motherly obligations to the full.
> :—)
> THANK YOU.

> From: Polly Wood
> To: Kate Reardon
> Sent: Friday, July 24, 2009 10:40 AM
> Subject: Re: Re: finished
>
> Ah yes. Slipped my mind.

index

tips for new mothers, 56, 74,
    105, 108–9, 128, 168–71, 226
travel tips, 175, 239, 276, 278,
    280
parents. *See* family; parenting
pelvic floor exercises, 61
pets, 190–200
    birds, 191
    cats, 120, 191–93
    dogs, 193, 194–98
    horses and ponies, 198–200
    rabbits, 200
photographs, 157, 204, 221, 222
    online profiles, 225
    wedding photos, 295
plastic wrap rolls, 43
play dough, 181
posture, 12, 249, 302
prank phone calls, 156–57
pregnancy
    health tips, 105, 109–10
    pregnant friends, 74, 75, 76,
        81–82

recycling tips, 47–48, 257–58
relationships, 201–32. *See also*
    family; men; weddings
    anniversaries, 225
    birthdays, 80–81
    cheating, 77, 211–13
    commitment, 213–14
    communications, 206, 214–15
    dating, 201, 216–20, 225, 235
    dealing with your ex, 220, 221,
        222–24
    ending, 204, 205, 208–11, 212,
        223–24

friendships and romantic
    interest, 67–68, 224
keeping things exciting,
    228–29
men and money, 203
miscellaneous tips, 202, 204,
    205, 207–8, 228
new partners and grown
    children, 54–55, 57–58, 222
pregnancy/birth and, 109–10,
    226
problems and doubts, 205–6,
    210
sex and kissing, 229–32
unwanted attention, 67–68,
    275–76, 299–300
Valentine's Day, 82
when you're older, 248, 251–53
your children's relationships,
    54, 187, 188
your friends' relationships, 77
your partner's children, 227
your partner's ex, 221, 222, 227
your partner's parents, 52–53
renting an apartment, 138
rudeness, 69–70, 143, 144

safety tips, 139, 233–40, 254
    cars and driving, 237–38, 279
    children's safety, 182, 239
    computers and online safety,
        235, 269, 270, 272–73
    home, 236–37
    while traveling, 239, 240
salesmen, 143
saving money, 161, 163, 165. *See
    also* budget tips

ABOUT KATE REARDON

KATE REARDON has spent more than twenty years at the cutting edge of women's publishing. She started her career at nineteen as a fashion assistant at American *Vogue* and at twenty-one was made fashion editor of *Tatler*. She has contributed to most of the major British newspapers and written three columns in the *Times*— which named her one of Britain's best writers. She is currently a contributing editor at *Vanity Fair*. She lives in London during the week and goes to her cottage in Wiltshire on the weekends. She is saving up for a horse.